JUST WAR?

Just War?

Charles Reed

CHURCH PUBLISHING
New York

Church Publishing, Incorporated.
445 Fifth Avenue
New York, New York 10016

5 4 3 2 1

Contents

Acknowledgements

I am very grateful to all those who have contributed to this project. Special thanks go to Alex Wright, Al McFadyen and Peter Sedgwick, all of whom encouraged me to put pen to paper. I am also indebted to Ruth McCurry for persevering with this initiative despite earlier reservations. That these reservations were overcome was in no small part due to the editorial skills of David Skidmore whose attention to detail brought some degree of order to an otherwise chaotic manuscript. This book would not however have been possible without the support of my friends and family, not least Rebecca.

Foreword

Jean Bethke Elshtain

An important story of our epoch is the reemergence of the doctrine and theory of the just or justifiable war and its challenge to the widespread functional pacifism that has overtaken Christian bodies and denominations in the West. Sadly, the debates stirred by this reemergence often downplay or bracket the theological backdrop to just war and its status as the predominant way that Western Christians historically justified and criticized the use of force. Too, there is a marked reluctance to invoke just war theory—or to misstate it—within the worldwide community of Christians in the conviction that Christianity is inherently and foundationally pacifist. It follows that *any* recourse to coercive force on the part of governments within majority-Christian cultures constitutes a fall from grace, if not an outright betrayal of the Christian message and the teachings of Jesus of Nazareth.

So widespread is this latter view that many appear to believe the only alternative to pacifism is something akin to a holy war—as if there were no middle ground. The many proponents of crypto- or functional pacifism admit, grudgingly, that one can entertain the hypothetical possibility that there might arise an occasion for the justifiable deployment of force. Yet, somehow, no armed conflict, or the prospect of such, seems to pass muster, save as cases of "pure" humanitarian intervention. Most likely World War II was a justified war, the thinking continues, although the Allies committed various infractions, even "war crimes," with the strategic bombing of German cities and the use of the atomic bombs on Hiroshima and Nagasaki. This fact didn't make "us" as bad as "them" in World War II, but it means that *just cause,* or *jus ad bellum,* recedes into the backdrop as *just* or *unjust means, jus in bello,* on the part of the anti-Hitler coalition is foregrounded.

Since the conclusion of World War II, however, the trend has been away from just war and toward the *de facto* if not *de jure* pacifism I have already noted. Predictable consequences followed, including the sorts of bankrupt "moral equivalence" claims that marred so many words uttered from the pulpit in the United States, at least, during the run-up to World War II. Within this framework, the difference between Hitler's Germany or Churchill's England or Franklin Delano Roosevelt's America was alleged to be in degree only, not kind.[1] Unsurprisingly, perhaps, a flurry of analogous declarations similarly marked many of the declarations and interventions by individual churchmen and women and denominational bodies throughout the Cold War. Yet again, we were told, the Cold War was a contestation between two aggressive imperial systems, each as guilty as the other-with the United States frequently taking the edge as the more aggressive of the two superpowers and most to blame for the Cold War. It was this strange, topsy-turvy view of matters that inspired Vaclav Havel, then a harried (and several times imprisoned) dissident, to note of the "peace groups" that visited the occupied countries of eastern Central Europe during the Cold War that they were unscrupulously naïve where the nature of Soviet domination was concerned. Writes Havel:

> . . . to Western peace fighters, the "dissidents" in the eastern half of central Europe must seem to be a people strangely absorbed in their provincial concerns, exaggerating human rights (as if human survival were not more important!), suspiciously prejudiced against the realities of socialism, if not against ideals themselves, people not sufficiently critical of Western democracy and perhaps even sympathizing, albeit secretly, with those detested Western armaments.[2]

A refusal to make critical distinctions—and that is what one sees in moral equivalence arguments—flies in the face of the just war tradition or dramatically resituates it, even in those circumstances in which just war is claimed as a framework. For the argument nearly all the time is that the use of coercive force is morally inferior to "soft power," and any resort to force, no matter the cause, constitutes a defeat for the pure Christian message, even in those situations in which resort to force is deemed a "least bad" alternative. Although political leaders and governments, certainly in the United

---

[1] See Joseph Laconte's fascinating collection, *The End of Illusions: Religious Leaders Confront Hitler's Gathering Storm* (Lanham, Md.: Rowman and Littlefield, 2004), for a generous sampling of the moral equivalence arguments within mainline Protestantism especially.

[2] Jan Vladislav, ed., *Vaclav Havel or Living in Truth: 22 Essays Published on the Occasion of the Award of the Erasmus Prize to Vaclav Havel* (London: Faber and Faber, 1987), 164-65.

States and the United Kingdom, have, and frequently do, frame discussions of the use of force within a just war framework, the churches, whether mainline Protestant, Roman Catholic, or Anglican, drift further and further away from just war and into the fold of crypto-pacifism.

This is where matters stood—until recently. Over the past few years, as I observed in my opening comments, we have witnessed a vigorous revival of the theological and historical warrants for just war teaching within the Christian tradition. Charles Reed's lucid and compelling book joins this company. The presuppositions that undergird his effort hold that Christians not only need to recover their own past and reinterpret its rich tradition of thinking about the use of force, they have the further responsibility to engage the dramatically altered circumstances in which we find ourselves post-1989 and post-9/11. Something rather more complex than slogans like "wage reconciliation" are called for. As I point out in my recent book, *Just War against Terror,* if one confronts international terrorism of the al-Qaeda variety there is no one accountable party to "wage" anything with. Osama bin Laden has made it clear that only the full defeat of all "Christians, Crusaders, and Zionists" will satisfy him. How one reconciles oneself to that, or develops even a stalemate, is unclear.

In an era when violent nonstate actors can inflict terrible and intentional damage on the innocent—those in no position to defend themselves in just war thinking—we are called upon to gather the richest, most complex, and most unblinking resources we can from our tradition. "Rediscovering the just war tradition," Reed calls it, and with this text he makes his own powerful contribution to this end. In his words:

> The just war tradition both in natural law and Christian theology has been developed through a continuing dialogue between secular and religious sources. The interaction between diverse and competing actors, including theologians, military commanders, and politicians, means that the just war tradition cannot be reduced to a set of moral assumptions or ideals. (p. 32)[3]

---

[3] And this is exactly what the most influential thinker in Christian pacifism over the last thirty years, John Howard Yoder, reduces the just war tradition to—as if it were a species of deontology rather than a complex product of the tradition of casuistry requiring the use of practical reason. See, for example, Yoder's *When War Is Unjust: Being Honest in Just-War Thinking* (Maryknoll, N.Y.: Orbis Books, 1996).

As Reed correctly notes, the just war tradition keeps alive what he calls the "ambiguity of Scripture" in the Christian tradition. Contrary to popular pacifist and crypto-pacifist claims, neither the holy texts of Christianity nor the early Christian community were unambiguously and consistently pacifist: the story is far more complex. As Reed notes, "Literal interpretations of the Bible that give rise to either a dogmatic militarism or pacifism tend to falsify Scripture by seeing it as amounting to a set of timeless instructions rather than as a set of historical documents reflecting the age in which it was written" (p. 29).

Just war thinking sustains deep moral argument and reflection on occasions for the use of force, including those searing moments when the greater sin by far would be to refrain from taking up arms in order to spare the innocent from certain harm. At the same time, just war restrains means and challenges triumphalist aspirations and temptations. This is a nuanced and demanding tradition, and that fact alone may help to account for why it is easier for many spokespersons from so many Christian denominations to wash their hands of the whole messy business and to link their views instead to a vision of a "pure" Christianity. It follows that the arguments of those embracing just war are downgraded and even condemned as an unacceptable capitulation. Yet just war endures as our most compelling way to attempt to steer a course between doctrinaire or crypto-pacifism, on the one hand, and ruthless Realpolitik that brackets ethical questions concerning the use of force, on the other.

With this work, Charles Reed offers a lively, challenging, highly readable contribution to a critical debate. Because we need all the wisdom we can get as we face the challenges of the present moment, his book is welcome indeed.

1 | Reflecting on War: Politics, Power and Religion in the New World Order

We were all reared on battles between great warriors, between great nations, between powerful forces. These were struggles for conquest, for land or money. The wars were fought by massed armies. The leaders were openly acknowledged: the outcomes decisive. Today, none of us expect our soldiers to fight a war on our territory. The immediate threat is not war between the world's powerful nations. The threat comes because . . . a new and deadly virus has emerged. The virus is terrorism, whose intent to inflict destruction is unconstrained by human feeling; and whose capacity to inflict it is enlarged by technology. This is a battle that can't be fought or won only by armies. Our ultimate weapon is not our guns but our beliefs.

(Tony Blair, Speech to the US Congress, 18 July 2003)

This book examines the way in which the British churches sought to offer wise moral counsel to governments and wider society on issues of war and peace following the end of the Cold War. Two trends dominate this book. The first is the increasing secularization of British society and the subsequent marginalization of God and of God-talk within society and politics. The second is the radical transformation in the way that states view and use military force as an instrument of foreign policy. To understand how British churches have reacted to, and were affected by, these trends this book focuses on those political debates that characterized the international crisis between Iraq and the international community during the years 1990 to 2003. In analysing that experience the book will also ask how far the liberal Protestant tradition – associated particularly with Reinhold Niebuhr – remained influential in the churches' contribution to discussions on war and peace.

There have been previous studies of the British churches' wartime experience. Alan Wilkinson's *The Church of England and the First World War* and his more recent publication *Dissent or Conform: War,*

Peace and the English Churches 1900–1945 examine the churches' search for moral clarity and meaning in time of war.[1] There have also been reflective studies such as William Temple's *Thoughts in War-Time*, or biographies examining the contribution of particular church leaders to the wartime ministry of the Church.[2] Other publications document the churches' contribution to the debate over the morality of nuclear deterrence during the Cold War period; but few studies examine the contribution of the UK churches to foreign policy discussions since 1989. While Kenneth Vaux examines the use of religious imagery and rhetoric at the time of the 1990 Gulf War, other studies concentrate on particular strands of Christian thinking like the just war tradition or pacifism.[3]

This study attempts to fill this gap by revisiting, in the light of the policy of the international community towards Iraq, 1990–2003, some of the conclusions reached by Wilkinson in his study of English churches' attitudes to war and peace between 1900 and 1945. Wilkinson makes a strong criticism:

> English churches have been humiliated and rendered impotent by their failure to exercise prophetic discernment about the questions that affect the lives of ordinary people. The most obvious example of this has been the failure of the churches to do or say anything distinctively Christian about war.[4]

By studying the churches' contribution over a 13-year period conclusions can be drawn as to how churches have reacted to the changed political climate ushered in by the end of the Cold War. The simplicity of the Cold War has been replaced by developments associated with a 'hot peace', which has led to a revision of the norms of international relations. The challenge to traditional thinking about security is clear from such developments as humanitarian intervention, intra-state conflict, terrorism, rogue regimes and the proliferation of weapons of mass destruction.

Iraq provides a valuable case study for the evaluation of the churches' contribution to political discussions about the ethics of military force in the post-Cold War era. No other issue has so dominated the international agenda in that period. It has engaged the enduring attention of governments, international institutions, military strategists and civil society in a debate about minimum standards of behaviour which can be demanded of any state which expects to be treated as a member of the international community. Central to this debate has been the formulation of criteria that a community will use in determining when to employ force, whether military or economic, to ensure that such standards are observed by defaulters. If the 1990–91 Gulf War gave rise to the idea of a 'New World Order', the 2003 Gulf War gave it renewed meaning.

The international community's engagement with Iraq has been shaped by fundamental changes taking place in global politics, such as the end of the Cold War and the terrorist attacks of 11 September 2001. Moreover, the precedents set in Iraq have in turn helped to shape the continued evolution of the international system. The conflict has raised questions that have been at the very heart of contemporary international affairs since the end of the Cold War.

Iraq has often appeared as part of a subplot within a wider play whose central theme is the definitive end of the post-Cold War interregnum and the opening up of the US imperial moment. The question of how the international community accommodates US hegemony in a post-Cold War era dominated this period. As Tony Blair remarked on the eve of the Second Gulf War:

> the outcome of this issue will determine the way that Britain and the world confront the central security threat of the Twenty First Century, the development of the United Nations, the relationship between Europe and the United States, the relations within the European Union and the way that the United States engages with the rest of the world.[5]

It could be argued that there had been no turning point of comparable importance since the end of the Second World War, which gave rise to NATO, the UN and what was to become the EU. Underpinning political debates about the use of force against Iraq has been the wider question of the type of world order which is to be secured through the use of force.

Not surprisingly, therefore, Iraq 1990–2003 has generated an unprecedented level of public and political debate. The growing interdependence of states means that the nation state can no longer be seen as the sole actor on the stage of world events. There is now a plethora of actors such as international and regional institutions, diaspora communities, pressure groups, religious communities and movements which all compete with government in an area traditionally reserved for the nation state.

Studying the Iraq debate, over a 13-year period, provides an opportunity to draw conclusions as to how governments make decisions about whether or not to use their military forces, when they have to design policies aimed at satisfying a broader audience under the constant scrutiny of public opinion. Yet by focusing on the British churches, as just one set of actors among the many within an emerging civil society, it is hoped to clarify the nature of this civil society, and the manner in which it impacts upon a state's ability to exercise good judgement in foreign policy. As one international relations expert, Christopher Hill, observed, 'civil society, the state and the values which they serve are shapers of foreign policy and may be shaped by it in turn'.[6]

Given the increased complexity of international politics, both in terms of the issues facing governments as well as the multiple actors that they have to contend with, how is a debate between government and civil society structured and maintained? Similarly, aware that churches are not themselves homogenous actors, how do churches structure their dialogue with their own constituent members, some of whom hold positions of influence and responsibility within society and politics. Politicians like Tony Blair, Gordon Brown and Iain Duncan Smith are after all lay people of their own churches and as such they are the main embodiment of the churches' theology and teaching.

One of the significant characteristics of this debate, it may be suggested, whether it relates to the First Gulf War, sanctions or the Second Gulf War, has been the extent to which it has been framed in terms of the moral criteria and political logic associated with the just war tradition. Politicians, government ministers, senior military analysts, church leaders, media pundits and ordinary citizens have debated the goals and instruments of UK foreign policy towards Iraq in such classic terms as 'just cause', 'competent authority', 'probability of success', 'last resort', 'right intent', 'proportionality' and 'discrimination'.

Language has always been important in politics, but what exactly do these just war terms mean? More specifically, in a society in which religious belief appears to have very limited influence, what meaning can be attached to 'just war' language which has traditionally been associated with theologians and church leaders? The use of just war terminology does not, of course, represent evidence of a religious revival in the UK, but the phenomenon is nonetheless striking and needs explanation. Does the revival of the just war tradition point to a more value-based approach to foreign policy? If so, how relevant is a tradition, first developed some twelve hundred years ago, in offering criteria for deciding how new security issues can be appropriately dealt with?

This book addresses these issues and draws conclusions as to the value of just war theory in providing a framework for churches (and the political, military and academic elites they seek to influence) in making judgements about the morality of using force in particular situations. It is argued that because the just war tradition has developed through a dialogue between secular and religious sources, it can offer something more valuable than a set of moral assumptions and ideals. It has shaped methods of statecraft and rules of military engagement while still providing guidance to individuals grappling with the ethical choices associated with war. It represents a public theology, grounded in Western culture and shaped by historical experience, which provides churches, as one of many actors, with a legitimate public space in which to reflect deeply on the ethics of war even within a largely secularized society.

There are a number of interrelated questions. What 'degree of moral wisdom' did British churches bring to the Iraq debate?[7] Did British religious institutions 'help nurture and deepen a genuinely public moral argument, or did they simply advance preconceived political – indeed partisan – agendas dressed up in the language of morality and religious conviction?'[8] Did they display signs of institutional learning during the 1990s that enabled them to develop an effective contribution to the public debate on Iraq? Answers to these questions rest not only on an analysis of how churches used the just war tradition at any given time, but also on how they responded to the changed international environment ushered in by the end of the Cold War and the terrorist attacks of 11 September 2001.

James Turner Johnston and George Weigel asked these questions of US religious responses to the 1990–91 Gulf War.[9] Their conclusions suggest that US churches abandoned their most precious slogan, that of peace with justice, in favour of a debased and morally suspect concept: peace as the mere absence of violence. Weigel wrote: 'Unhappily, it cannot be said that the formal leadership of the American religious community brought very much wisdom on matters of ethics and international affairs to the debate, before, during and after the Persian Gulf War.'[10] Individual denominations, like the US Catholic Bishops' Conference and the Episcopal (Anglican) Church in the USA, were seen by such critics as abdicating their role of public educator, by showing themselves incapable of providing the kind of public moral leadership they had usually exercised in American society.

Central to the criticisms levelled at mainline denominations was the charge that the USA could have benefited from a religiously grounded peace movement during the Gulf War to assist it in clarifying the debate over the ends and means of US power in the post-Cold War world. For central to the debate was the question of the kind of peace that was being sought for the Middle East by the deployment of US troops. The failure of US churches to meet this challenge flowed from their profound alienation from the US experiment and a deep conviction that US power cannot be a force for good in the world.

This psychology, it was argued, reflected the mistrust of US military power following the Vietnam War. The Vietnam experience conditioned church leaders to approach issues of war and peace from a particular pacifist viewpoint reflective of their own political activism during the 1960s. In exchange for a Christian realism of the kind expounded by Reinhold Niebuhr, church leaders were seen to substitute a 'curdled hash composed in part of unvarnished *Tercermundismo* and in part of a neo-isolationist version of precisely that liberal Protestant sentimentality against which Niebuhr had inveighed'.[11]

This book uses the moral reasoning developed by US theologians such as Paul Ramsey, James Turner Johnston and George Weigel to critically analyse the British churches' contribution to the political debate surrounding Iraq in the 1990s. There are both striking differences and similarities between the UK and the United States of America, which make such a study interesting and valuable. While there is no established church in the USA, and although the separation of 'church' and 'state' is fiercely protected, the USA is by any standard a deeply religious society. Although the academic debate around the 'secularization thesis' has been intense in relation to Britain there can be little dispute that, at least in the public sphere, there has been a marked marginalization of the Church, of God and of God-talk.[12] Despite this trend the United Kingdom has an established church, which places the Church of England as part of the establishment.

Regardless of the arguments for or against such an arrangement, the Church of England occupies what may seem to be a privileged position relative to other churches. The question to be explored here is the degree to which the Church of England used its privileged position to contribute to the public debate on Iraq what Weigel has termed 'wise moral guidance'. Did the position of the Church of England differ radically from positions adopted by other British churches? If so, why? Whatever the institutional position of the churches, how influential were the British churches, in shaping the public and political debate on Iraq? Did their advice easily commend itself to policy-makers or did they promote arguments 'that tend to sail on general ideas rather than on a concrete analysis of what politicians are actually able to do'?[13]

A brief outline may be helpful. Chapter 2 examines the authority by which the churches contribute to public policy discussions on such points as the appropriate use of force within international affairs. It is suggested that the ambiguity of Scripture has given rise to competing answers to the moral questions raised by war and peace. The just war tradition developed as a means by which the extremes of pacifism or militarism might be avoided. Chapter 3 examines the just war tradition, its origins and development, and recent ethical and political debates which have occurred since the end of the Cold War. Particular attention is paid to the impact of these debates on the just war tradition. Do developments since the end of the Cold War render the just war tradition redundant?

Chapters 4 and 5 examine how the British churches reacted to the First and Second Gulf Wars, both in terms of events and in their use of the just war tradition. How did the churches respond to the tumultuous events of the fall of the Berlin Wall and the terrorist attacks of 11 September 2001? How did these events affect their use of the just war tradition? What can be learnt from these wars as to the nature of church–state relations and church–society relations in contemporary Britain? In the light of this analysis, Chapter 6 suggests the lessons that need to be learnt if churches, the moral guardian of the just war tradition, are to respond effectively to changes in international relations.

2 | War and the Ambiguity of Scripture

I am for peace, but when I speak of it they make themselves ready for war.

(Psalm 120.7)

Many studies have explored the justification for the churches' contribution to public policy discussions.[1] Among the most recent is Anthony Harvey's *By What Authority?* Harvey poses the crucial question: 'What basis exists in the Christian faith for making authoritative judgements on matters such as genetic engineering or financial policy which clearly lie well outside the scope of the historic religious traditions?'[2]

Harvey's focus of study was on reports such as *Faith in the City* and *Unemployment and the Future of Work*, written in the last quarter of the twentieth century.[3] However, the focus of this chapter is on the specific area of the theological or philosophical basis which informs the churches' understanding of and contribution to public discussions on war and peace. Have the reports dealing with these themes over the years, such as *Force in the Modern World*, *Christians in a Violent World*, *The Church and the Bomb* and *Peacemaking in a Nuclear Age*, offered a unique Christian perspective on war distinct from the pre-existing moral consensus?

Common to all these documents are the recommendations that churches make to Government. Churches consciously promote their own understanding of how governments ought to act in any given situation. These documents therefore reflect not only the churches' philosophical and theological traditions on such issues, but also the assumption that the insights offered by a Christian understanding of politics can be commended to Government. The amount of paper produced by churches at times of international crisis suggests that churches believe that they not only have some-thing worth saying, but that what they say should help inform foreign policy considerations. Churches assume there is a role for ethics, and especially a Christian ethic, within foreign policy calculations.

In this chapter we examine those theological traditions that have shaped the churches' understanding of war and peace and in particular those discussions of war and peace that have dominated the agenda since the end of the Cold War. While certain passages of Scripture support the particular positions of pacifists and non-pacifists alike, the Bible should not be seen as a 'maker's handbook' with a set of timeless instructions for being human, but a collection of historical documents written thousands of years ago.[4] Whatever moral authority is ascribed to it, the Bible clearly requires a continual and lengthy process of interpretation.

This need for interpretation accounts for the different theological assessments of war and peace. Between Old Testament militarism and New Testament pacifism stands the just war tradition, which has shaped much Christian thinking on war since the time of St Augustine. Advocates of this tradition believe that the criteria it sets out can be commended to politicians and policy-makers as a practical guide to contemporary international relations.

Old Testament militarism – a lesson in internecine war

On 1 September 1689 the Revd Cotton Mather preached his sermon *Soldiers Counselled and Comforted* to those soldiers engaged in the conflict with the native inhabitants of New England. The sermon is striking for its rich use of Old Testament imagery to justify the war. Mather argued that the indigenous population were a legitimate target because they had murdered Christians. Yet, Mather goes beyond this assertion to portray the enemy as Ammon and Amalek, an indigenous population, which needed to be defeated in order to make way for the 'New Israel'.

Mather's political use of Old Testament imagery is not unique. Similar imagery was used to justify the crusades. During the English Civil War the Hebrew Scriptures were also used to justify the use of force.[5] This approach to the Old Testament has led one Old Testament scholar, Susan Niditch, to write: 'The particular violence of the Hebrew scriptures has inspired violence, has served as a model of, and a model for persecution, subjugation, and extermination for millennia beyond its own reality.'[6]

Most chilling within the Old Testament are those biblical texts relating to *herem,* the ban under which all those defeated, combatants and non-combatants alike, were put to death. The God of the Hebrew Scriptures that commands 'thou shall not kill' (Exodus 20.13), is the same God that violently overthrows the Pharaohs in order to liberate his people from the slavery of Egypt (Exodus 14), so that they could occupy by force the land beyond the Jordan (Joshua 8). This is the same God that legitimized the Israelites' extermination of indigenous populations so as to avoid any contamination with pagan religious practices (Deuteronomy 20.17). Similarly, 2 Kings 24.10–17 sanctions death, enslavement and the plunder of a city after a siege.

There are other less brutal models of Old Testament warfare. The First and Second Books of Chronicles portray the Israelites as a humbled people forced to call on God's assistance in their hour of need. This image of God as 'liberator' is central to the Israelites' history, as illustrated by their exodus from Egypt. This model of war, involving as it does the idea of non-participation, or outside participation, characterizes the battle with Amalek (Exodus 17.8–13) and the siege of Jericho (Joshua 6.20). These wars are not some early variant of Christian pacifism, for the image of God is still that of Yahweh the destroyer.

Between these extremes, there are wars described in Chronicles and Kings. These texts present an image of war reminiscent of the splendour of the *Iliad*. David's struggle with Goliath and the story of Gideon conjure up the imagery of bold warriors engaged in heroic struggles (1 Samuel 17.38–51; Judges 6.12). War is seen as sport in which men pit their skills and strength against one another. There are discernible rules to the game, a code of fair play, providing instructions as to what constitutes acceptable wartime behaviour. Guidance is offered on how the spoils of war should be divided (Joshua 22.8) and on the appropriate care of prisoners during war (2 Chronicles 28; 2 Kings 6.22–23). Some Old Testament scholars believe these texts constitute 'the outlines of a just war code especially pertaining to *jus in bello,* a code of conduct shared by fighters on the same side and by enemies'.[7]

Common to all these accounts of warfare is the image of Yahweh, the God who wages war, has favourites and protects only his own. As Harvey writes:

In the Hebrew scriptures there is no doubt whatever that God is a God of battles, a God who 'goes out with our armies' – a theology which has given great reassurance to the leaders of countless military enterprises who have confidently proclaimed that God was on their side. No amount of sophisticated modern criticism can materially alter the overall impression given by these scriptures of a God who approves the use of force and is often invoked as the champion and protector of armed forces.[8]

These trends persisted throughout the twentieth century. Lloyd George laced his speeches with biblical allusions so as to manipulate the Free Churches into supporting the 1914–18 war.[9] In 1943 Winston Churchill described the allied war effort as a collection of warrior nations 'walking in fear of the Lord, very heavily armed and with an increasingly clear view of their salvation'.[10] Religious leaders have not been immune from this trend. During the Second World War, the Bishop of London, the Rt Revd Arthur Winnington-Ingram, stated: 'You ask for my advice in a sentence as to what the Church is to do. I answer mobilise the nation for a holy war.'[11]

The Old Testament imagery of warfare has parallels with contemporary international relations. It illustrates the uncertainty and risk associated with military endeavours as well as the extent of human casualties associated with warfare. There are similarities between the wars of Deuteronomy and the struggles of the post-Cold War period. Even if the historical accuracy of these wars remains in doubt, the texts provide insights into the writers' world-views which continue to resonate in the twenty-first century.

The USA – the redeemer nation

Karen Rasmussen and Sharon Downey show that throughout its history the USA has seen wars as cleansing struggles in pursuit of holy victory. War is a 'sacred purifying, culturally regenerative quest for victory against a sinister foe'.[12] President Bush's 1992 State of the Union Speech argued that the USA's greatness rested on its ability to seek out and destroy enemies of civilization, whether it be 'imperial communism or nationalism'. Only the steadfastness of the USA's moral vision had secured the post-Cold War peace. Crucial to this peace was the 'idea of America' as the last best hope of humanity.

President Bush believed the USA had been granted divine sanction for its role as the 'undisputed leader of the age', where it alone would act as the world's police force and the guardian of democracy and freedom.[13] There are clear Old Testament overtones between the idea of the USA as the 'chosen nation', the 'New Israel', and the vision of war as an instrument of purification.

The use of Old Testament imagery in US foreign policy has become more pronounced following the terrorist attacks of 11 September 2001. President Bush's rhetoric presented the war in Afghanistan as a moral 'crusade' involving a battle between 'good' and 'evil'. His State of the Union Speech on 29 January 2001, declaring that an 'axis of evil', consisting of Iraq, Iran and North Korea, threatened world peace and security, was reminiscent of Ronald Reagan's description of the Soviet Union as the 'evil empire'.[14] This use of such language in relation to the war on terrorism reminds the Islamic world, in particular, of the marauding Christian armies of medieval times.[15]

Bush's crusade can be seen as reflecting a long tradition in US foreign policy where wars are portrayed as being fought in favour of democracy and more recently human rights. The promotion of democracy abroad, even if in practice it leads to its repression, can be traced back to the 1898 Spanish–American war. This war ended with the USA 'trying to establish democratic governments locally, and then departing'.[16] The aggressive pursuit of democracy and the right to self-determination characterized Woodrow Wilson's Fourteen Points after the First World War. It was the cornerstone of President Truman's Marshall Plan after the Second World War. During the Cold War the defence of liberty against the perceived communist threat took precedence. This did not prevent the USA from encouraging European states to dismantle their empires. Following the end of the Cold War the promotion of democratic internationalism once again became more pronounced.[17] It has seen interventions in Iraq, Somalia, Bosnia, Kosovo and Afghanistan. It is of course paradoxical that intervening to provide the conditions necessary for democracy and nation-building has required on occasions the temporary suspension of democracy in favour of direct rule from Washington.[18]

Although this moral crusade promotes 'universal' values like democracy and human rights, elements within US society, most notably the New Christian Right, have sought to use this postmodern crusade to promote an agenda which is pre-modern inasmuch as it explicitly rejects the Enlightenment legacy. The New Christian Right comprises Southern Baptists, Pentecostals, Evangelicals and charismatic religious movements. All trace their history through Puritanism and the Great Revival Movement of the nineteenth century. Found mainly within America's Southern Bible belt, it represents 'traditional people struggling to maintain rural religious values in an increasingly urban and secular society'. [19]

The New Christian Right follows a redemptive pattern in politics and places a heavy emphasis on conversion, both politically and spiritually. This 'born-again politics' promotes passionate and uncompromising moral messages, such as the need to combat abortion, homosexuality and pornography.[20] Their language is at times apocalyptic. Paul Weyrich saw the campaign to outlaw abortion as 'the most significant battle of the age-old battle between good and evil, between the forces of God and the forces against God that we have seen in our country'.[21]

This apocalyptic language also characterizes the New Christian Right's world-view. For them Christianity has an inbuilt gospel imperative to carry the Christian message to all parts of the world. It subscribes politically to a strong brand of patriotism, where the USA is seen to have responsibility for bringing law and order to other parts of the world. The USA is the redeemer nation, singled out by God as part of his providential plan. In *The Light and the Glory*, Peter Marshall and David Manuel write: 'In the virgin wilderness of America, God was making His most significant attempt since ancient Israel to create a new Israel of people living in obedience to the laws of God, through faith in Jesus Christ.'[22]

Anti-communism was a fundamental article of faith for the New Christian Right. It found a political expression in Ronald Reagan's perception of the USSR as the 'evil empire'. John Eindsmore, an evangelical Christian, wrote:

> The informed Christian will realise that Communism is totally at odds with Christianity and is the greatest evil of the twentieth century. A biblically based foreign policy – indeed, the policy of any freedom loving nation – must be one of absolute and uncompromising opposition to Communism.[23]

This confrontational stance led to a coalition between religious and political conservatives which has encouraged the USA to retain its hegemonic position through the proliferation of conventional and unconventional weapons.

While the end of the Cold War and the Clinton presidency led to a decline in the political prominence of the New Christian Right, the movement used the period in which it had a lower profile to reassess its strategy and it re-emerged with the post-September 11 war against terrorism. President Bush, in a speech to the National Convention of Religious Broadcasters on 10 February 2003, stated: 'I welcome faith to solve the nation's deepest problems. We're being challenged. We're meeting those challenges because of our faith. We carried our grief to the Lord Almighty in prayer.'[24] The war against terrorism became a convenient vehicle through which the New Christian Right pressed the case for the USA once again to act as a redeemer nation. Not surprisingly the war against terrorism, with its potential to be perceived as part of a wider clash of civilizations, replaced anti-communism as the Christian Right's new moral crusade. Jerry Falwell, for instance, called the Prophet Muhammad a 'terrorist', while Pat Robertson described him a 'wild-eyed fanatic', a 'robber' and a 'brigand'. To Franklin Graham, the son of Billy Graham, Islam is a 'very evil and wicked religion', while Jerry Vines, a leading Southern Baptist, called the Prophet Muhammad a 'demon-obsessed paedophile'.[25]

In the eschatology of the New Christian Right Israel is the key. To many US evangelicals the complete restoration of Israel is a prerequisite for the 'second coming'. Any attempt at pressurizing successive Israeli administrations to make peace with the Palestinians by giving up any part of 'biblical' Israel is to be resisted. Thwarting Israel's ambitions to build a greater Israel is tantamount to thwarting God's master plan. As Jerry Falwell stated: 'God has blessed America because of our support for the state of Israel.'[26] That God's blessing comes at the expense of human rights abuses and the flouting of international law counts for little. Seen from this perspective there appear to be striking similarities between the use of Old Testament imagery by Mather in the seventeenth century and by Pat Robertson or Jerry Falwell in the twenty-first century.

Understanding the US world-view

The alliance between the New Christian Right and the neo-conservative elements within the Republican Party, and the use of biblical imagery to support foreign policy objectives, is indicative of a narrowly conceived realist perspective of international relations. Realism holds that national interest, unrestrained by moral constraints, should determine the conduct of war. While political realists would admit that some of the language of the Old Testament is offensive and that some of Joshua's actions would now be considered war crimes, they argue that when the fundamental interests of the state are threatened, state interests should prevail over moral considerations.[27] Central to realism is the assumption that states exist in an anarchical society, similar to a Hobbesian state of nature, in which a strict observance of legal and moral prohibitions against aggression might jeopardize a state's survival.[28]

The British historian E. H. Carr defined political realism as both a school of thought and a frame of action in the field of political decision-making.[29] As a school of thought realism emerged as a reaction against the idealism and utopianism of the inter-war years.[30] It recognized that the political world could not be remade according to human desires and moral aspirations. Adopting such a moral approach would invariably lead to failure, because it overlooked the inherent constraints under which decision-makers operate. These constraints include the circumstances of choice, the goals decision-makers hold and the resources available to them. These restrictions make it necessary for political decision-makers to sacrifice some of their ideals if they are to achieve any of their goals.

This perspective on politics has characterized much of US foreign policy since 1945. It is most commonly associated with the power politics of George Kennan and Henry Kissinger. It assumes that power, and the preservation of this power through the will to dominate others, is central to national interest. It holds there is an 'ineluctable tension', 'tragic antimony' and an 'unbridgeable gulf' between moral norms and the demands of effective political action.[31]

Elements of this doctrine were evident in the National Security Strategy of the United States of America, September 2002. It reflected Bush's belief that 'a President must be a clear-eyed realist'.[32] The starting point was the assumption that 'the US possesses unprecedented and unequalled strength and influence in the world' and that the primary thrust of foreign policy was to maintain this hegemony by 'dissuading future military competition, deterring threats against US interests and decisively defeating any adversary if deterrence fails'.[33]

The drive to maintain US hegemony has manifested itself in a number of ways. According to the US National Security Strategy, the USA cannot be institutionally constrained: 'While the United States will constantly strive to enlist the support of the international community, we will not hesitate to act alone, if necessary, to exercise our right of self-defence.'[34] Therefore, the USA will only participate in those multilateral organizations or alliances which enhance, rather than limit, its power. As Donald Rumsfeld, the US Secretary of State for Defence, remarked while building the international coalition against Afghanistan, in 2001: 'The mission should determine the coalition rather than the coalition determining the mission.'[35]

There are signs that this realist approach, which prioritizes the pursuit of national self-interest, has led to a devaluing of those international rules and agreements that have underpinned the international community since 1945. The USA's repudiation of the Kyoto Protocol, the International Criminal Court, the Comprehensive Test Ban Treaty and the Biological Weapons Convention all point to a unilateralist trend. The decision to increase the US defence budget to over $500 billion by 2010, to a level that surpasses anything spent in the Cold War, illustrates that in a post-September 11 world the ability to project military power remains a key feature of US foreign policy.[36] Whether the USA will be able to maintain such spending is a moot point, but it leaves little doubt that the US empire is one which involves the possession of overwhelming military power.

Christian realism – a lesson in political pragmatism

Writers such as Reinhold Niebuhr, John Bennett and Ernest Lefever provide a moral variant on this more extreme version of realism, but one still rooted in the Old Testament account of the fall. Contextually, Christian realism emerged as a response to the radical economic and political changes of the inter-war years, such as the 1929 Wall Street crash, mass unemployment and the rise of fascism and communism across Europe. Theologically it was a reaction against the social gospel movement, which regarded human nature as changeable and part of an evolutionary progress towards the realization of the Kingdom of God.[37] John Atherton argues that like the social gospel movement that grew out of a response to industrialization and urbanization as well as a highly individualistic theology of the nineteenth century, Christian realism was a reaction against the context of, and deficiencies in, liberal social theology in the 1920s.[38]

On this understanding, Christian realism emerged as an attempt to find a third way between the optimism of the social gospel movement and the pessimism of Karl Barth's and Emil Brunner's new orthodoxy. As a methodology Christian realism 'denotes the disposition to take all factors in a social and political situation, which offers resistance to established norms, into account, particularly the factors of self-interest and power'.[39] The inescapable characteristics of human reality are seen as a capacity for concern for others, combined with a tendency towards selfishness and domination.

Christian realism holds that the behaviour of nation states is similar to that of human nature, in that behaviour is motivated by self-interest.[40] This self-interest can, however, sometimes coincide with the global interest, in that nations are bound by a common quest for peace and justice. Christian realism recognizes that finding a common good remains problematic, if not impossible, given the competition between social groups which compromise any polity. For this reason Niebuhr recognized:

> a sharp distinction must be drawn between the moral and social behaviour of individuals and of social groups, national, racial, economic; and that this distinction justifies and necessitates political policies which a purely individualistic ethic must always find embarrassing.[41]

This understanding of human nature and its impact upon the workings of any social grouping leads Christian realists to reject the idea that the Christian ideal of love can overcome the reality of sin. There is therefore no direct step from the ethics of Jesus to the political realm.[42] Niebuhr writes:

> The ethics of Jesus does not deal at all with the immediate moral problem of every human life – the problem of arranging some kind of armistice between various contending factions

and forces. It has nothing to say about the relativities neither of politics and economics nor of the necessary balances of power that exist and must exist in even the most intimate social relationships.[43]

Jesus' ethic relates to the person and not to the body politic. The instructions to 'love your enemies and pray for those who persecute you' (Matthew 5.44), and 'do not resist evil'. (Matthew 5.39) fall within the private rather than the public sphere of responses and attitudes. The Christian ideal of love is an impossible ethical ideal. It remains unrealized because humanity cannot escape the consequences of sin.

Christian realism attempts to overcome this dilemma by emphasizing the need for 'an ascending scale of moral possibilities', on which the best approximation of the Christian ideal of love is justice.[44]

> The problem of politics and economics is the problem of justice. The question of politics is how to coerce the anarchy of conflicting human interests into some kind of order, offering human beings the greatest possible opportunity for mutual support.[45]

The challenge is to curb the worst excesses of human behaviour while promoting the well-being of humanity. As a result, 'the Christian faith stands between the illusions and the despair of the world; it is particularly an antidote to the illusions which are stubbornly held in defiance of the facts in order to save men from despair'.[46]

Christian realism holds to a view of international relations where the 'national interest' is not necessarily without moral or intellectual power. Lefever suggests: 'Each nation can be said to have a national purpose, a reason for its existence, which is based upon the central values, held by the majority of its people. The government is morally bound to honour these basic values.'[47] The problem for governments is 'to choose between their own immediate, perhaps too narrowly conceived, interests and the common interests of their alliance, or more ultimately of their civilisation, in which, of course, their "national interest" is also involved'.[48] Finding the points of concurrence between the two is therefore not 'just the art of statecraft, it is the moral duty of all involved in national policy'.[49]

Christian realism has generated an ethic of international politics, which recognizes that while there are natural limits to the role of morality within politics, morality cannot be divorced from politics.

> An adequate political morality must do justice to the insight of both moralists and political realists. It will recognise that human society will never escape social conflict, even though it extends the areas of social co-operation. It will try to save society from being involved in endless cycles of futile conflict not by an effort to abolish coercion in the life of collective man, but by reducing it to a minimum, by counselling the use of such types of coercion as are most compatible with the moral and rational factors in human society, and by distinguishing between the purposes and ends for which coercion is used.[50]

The challenge to Christian realists is to find a moral yet realistic approach to politics that recognizes, but ameliorates, the tension between Christian ethics and the requirements of political success.

The political utility of Christian realism

Although Christian realism has not generated a movement similar to pacifism, it has nonetheless featured heavily in political calculations. Reinhold Niebuhr's time as consultant to George Kennan's Policy Planning Staff in the US State Department meant he was fully aware of the complexities of making ethical decisions. It was his ability to develop an ethically relevant political world-view which so commended him and Christian realism to politicians. US politicians such as Adlai Stevenson, McGeorge Bundy and Hubert Humphrey all acknowledged the influence of Christian realism in general and Reinhold Niebuhr in particular. Even President Clinton is said to have acknowledged Reinhold Niebuhr as a significant political influence.[51]

Despite President Bush's tendency to reject all Clintonite policies and methodologies, it is nonetheless possible to identify elements of Christian realism in US foreign policy since 2001. The 2002 US National Security Strategy stated: 'the US does not seek to use its strength to press for unilateral advantage'. Instead, the purpose of US power is 'to create a balance of power that favours human freedom in which all nations and all societies can choose for themselves the rewards and challenges of political and economic liberty'.[52]

There is a missionary zeal – even a moralistic streak – to the 2002 Strategy paper, which contrasts with most understandings of realism. It suggests a directional and progressive approach to history where good can overcome evil. This faith stems from President Bush's own born-again Christian experience, which fuels a transformative political world-view. Promoting global norms like freedom, human rights and democracy suggests that it is possible to escape the anarchical international society 'to build a world where great powers compete in peace instead of continually preparing for war'.[53] What makes this possible is that countries are 'increasingly united by common values'.

While the USA may on occasion aggressively promote these global norms through military means, the end result is an imperial system based around common values rather than any imperialistic quest for territorial self-aggrandizement. It is an empire based on an idea rather than on territory, but one that relies on military means to uphold and defend it. Paradoxically, it echoes the Wilsonian interventionism of the early twentieth century. Mazarr writes: 'This is a missionary, idealistic administration in the best and sometimes worst traditions of Wilsonianism.'[54]

The influence of this approach can be seen elsewhere. It has influenced the thinking of British politicians such as Denis Healey, Tony Benn and Richard Crossman.[55] It has been seen in British foreign policy since 1997. Following the 1997 General Election, the new Labour Government unveiled its mission statement for the Foreign and Commonwealth Office.

> The Mission of the Foreign and Commonwealth Office is to promote the national interests of the United Kingdom and contribute to a strong international community . . . We shall pursue that Mission to secure for Britain four benefits (security, prosperity, the quality of life and mutual respect) . . . We shall work through our international relationships to spread the values of human rights, civil liberties and democracy, which we demand for ourselves.[56]

Robin Cook, the Foreign Secretary, subsequently reinforced this statement:

> The Labour Government does not accept that political values can be left behind when we check in our passports to travel on diplomatic business. Our foreign policy must have an ethical dimension and must support the demands of other peoples for the democratic rights on which we insist for ourselves. We will put human rights at the heart of our foreign policy.[57]

The Labour Government has promoted the idea of Britain as a 'force for good' in the world and as a 'good international citizen' adhering to and upholding a recognizable set of values. The trend characterized British foreign policy during the 1999 Kosovo conflict.

Tony Blair presented the NATO bombing of the Yugoslav Republic in the spring of 1999 as 'a just and moral cause', 'a just war, based not on any territorial ambitions but on values'.[58] In a speech to the Chicago Economic Club he spelt out his 'Doctrine of the International Community' in which 'we cannot let the evil of ethnic cleansing stand'. Blair went on to state:

> As we address these problems at this weekend's NATO Summit we may be tempted to think back to the clarity and simplicity of the Cold War. But now we have to establish a new framework. No longer is our existence as states under threat. Now our actions are guided by a more subtle blend of mutual self-interest and moral purpose in defending the values we cherish. In the end values and interest merge. If we can establish and spread the values of liberty, the rule of law, human rights and an open society then that is in our national interests too. The spread of our values makes us safer. As John Kennedy put it, 'freedom is indivisible and when one man is enslaved who is free at the end?'.[59]

Blair's idea of what constitutes an 'international community' is obviously value driven. It espouses the cause of internationalism, even cosmopolitanism, as against isolationism. Membership of the international community brings with it rights as well as responsibilities. Like Bush, Blair is willing to enforce certain global norms over and above state sovereignty. Both see sovereignty in conditional rather than absolutist terms and evidence of an emerging common good upheld by a core of like-minded states but in need of extension to those on the periphery.

This value-based approach is not without its critics or its dangers. There has always been a debate between those who argue that human rights derive from natural rights and are therefore universal rights, and those who are cultural relativists and so argue that individuals have rights only by virtue of the community to which they belong. Should Western values take precedence over Asian or even Islamic values?[60] Just because the West claims for itself these values, does it have a right to demand them of others as suggested by the 1997 UK mission statement? To what extent is the philosophy of universal human rights simply a reflection of the West's own Judaeo-Christian heritage? There is the danger that universalizing human rights can amount to a form of cultural imperialism. When countries use military means to secure human rights, they run the risk of being equated with the religious crusaders of old.

Although the Old Testament provides a contextual approach to war which is absent from the New Testament, it does not provide a model of warfare that would be acceptable today. Despite this limitation it is evident that the power politics of the Old Testament hold to a view of human nature which has given rise to a realist ethic which seeks a moral but realistic approach to politics. From a church-based perspective, such an ethic warns against making unrealistic demands of policy-makers and should make us sensitive to the constraints under which decision-makers operate. However, this approach has its critics. Some moral theologians like Philip Wogaman have argued that the national interest is too particular a starting point to fit the moral realities of a universal faith such as Christianity.[61] Indeed, to many Christians, political realism offers too pessimistic an account of human nature and one which is at odds with the optimism of the New Testament in general and the teachings of Jesus in particular.

The New Testament: grounds for human optimism

In the Sermon on the Mount Jesus says, 'love your enemies and pray for those who persecute you' (Matthew 5.44), and 'do not resist evil' (Matthew 5.39). He blesses the peacemakers and the meek (Matthew 5.5, 9). His warning, recorded elsewhere by Matthew, to those who take up the sword appears at first glance unequivocal (26.52). These teachings are brought to life by his own example of refusing to offer resistance to those who arrested and finally crucified him (1 Peter 2.23). Taken together these texts, it might be assumed, would suggest that Jesus would oppose war and any resort to violence.

Not surprisingly, many Christians have used these texts to argue that Christianity is a pacifist religion. Christian pacifism, so understood, urges Christians to live and act according to Christian standards as prescribed by the Bible. John Elford writes: 'Non violence is professed as an intrinsic moral duty which will not allow consideration of any consequences which would be contra-indicative.'[62] This approach characterizes such Christian traditions as those of the Quakers, Mennonites and Anabaptists, as well as abolitionist movements and those who sanction non-violent resistance. Despite their distinctiveness there has, in practice, been considerable cross-fertilization between the traditions.[63]

A variation on Christian pacifism is non-violent resistance, which renounces all uses of armed force on ethical grounds, but nonetheless holds that non-violent techniques exist to challenge aggression and injustice. Mahatma Gandhi's movement to liberate India from British rule by using the pacifist methods of *satyagraha* is often cited by Christian pacifists as testimony to the moral and political superiority of non-violent approaches to conflict transformation. The Velvet Revolutions of 1989–1990 are also given as examples of the political utility of non-violent approaches to conflict transformation.

Non-violent resistance has many theological advocates. John Yoder argues that Jesus' life and the manner of his death at the hands of the political authorities illustrates the viability of non-resistance as a political strategy.[64] Walter Wink has developed Yoder's thinking further with the idea of 'Jesus' third way'.[65] Central to Wink's argument is the proposition that Jesus was neither violent nor passive, rather he was actively good but locked in a perpetual struggle with the authorities. Wink's answer is for churches to rediscover Jesus' teachings and to commit themselves unambiguously to a non-violent agenda.[66]

Wink's general approach is shared by other strands of pacifism such as abolitionists who possess a strong moral commitment to work towards the eradication of war through the creation of a new international system. While this approach marked the Revd Dick

Sheppard's inter-war Peace Pledge Union, the origins of abolitionism can be traced as much to Immanuel Kant's *Perpetual Peace* as to any specifically Christian tradition.[67] Twentieth-century abolitionists were pacifists but with an internationalist agenda. They were both committed to, and encouraged by, developments such as the establishment of the League of Nations and later the United Nations. Abolitionist organizations like the World Policy Institute hoped that nation states would lose the right to use military force through the creation of a 'New World Order'.

Elements of this 'New World Order' are evident in European developments post-1945, where nation states have often eschewed the nineteenth-century balance of power theory in favour of a more co-operative decision-making model.

> The transnational states that constitute the world's first transnational community, the European Union, have established, in turn, the world's first transnational empire. It is an empire distinguished not by the use of military power, but other instruments of influence. Academics talk of a new diplomatic style cosmopolitanism.[68]

The postmodern European empire, built as it is on a growing community spirit, the *aquis communitaire*, provides for integration through negotiation, commercial ties and the extension of the rule of law. As Daniel Nelson puts it:

> Europe and the US dispute how states, institutions and communities act, or should act internationally. The implements and instruments of global action are from the US standpoint, those of power with a bit of co-operation. To Europeans, modalities have shifted significantly to co-operation and a discourse of Europe-ness with much less attention to power.[69]

Robert Cooper, a senior British diplomat and EU official, has argued that the European experiment rests not on the balance of power and the hegemonic aspirations of individual states but on the rejection of force and on self-enforced rules of behaviour.[70]

These European developments appear to some to suggest that European nation states have turned their back on the Hobbesian world of anarchy and embraced instead the Kantian world of perpetual peace.[71] They reflect a deep suspicion of the power of the state and its coercive powers both internally and externally. Taken to the extreme, seen in the writings of Noam Chomsky or, to a lesser degree, John Pilger, it can lead to a form of pacific globalism or revolutionary universalism. Their deep cynicism about the state denies the possibility that a state's action or behaviour can at any time be moral or ethical. This stance reflects some earlier twentieth-century Christian thinking such as that of the Roman Catholic moral philosopher Elizabeth Anscombe who subsequently argued that the 1939 war was not a just war because actions taken by Britain and France were too tainted by self-interest.[72]

Since the end of the Cold War there has developed a further strand of Christian witness centred on conflict prevention and conflict mediation. The end of the Cold War has seen the development of new security threats and challenges, which pose new ethical and political questions. Conflict today is often localized, involving two or more ethnic groupings in face-to-face combat often employing low-grade military equipment in such a way as to make the distinction between combatants and non-combatants irrelevant.[73]

Civil wars now rage in dozens of countries and are responsible for killing and displacing literally millions of people. Internal conflict was the most pervasive form of conflict in the international system during the 1990s. These intra-state conflicts evoked moral outrage at the perceived flouting of international law, especially in terms of the ethics of military engagement and the loss of distinction between combatants and non-combatants as set down in international law. In the most extreme cases these conflicts involved genocide on the scale seen in Bosnia and Rwanda.

Intra-state conflict offers new opportunities for Christian abolitionists as well as those that advocate a policy of non-violent conflict resolution. As John Lederach writes:

> The primary arena of Church activity and faith – that of the spiritual, emotional, and relational well being of people – lies at the heart of contemporary conflict . . . [W]here neighbour fears neighbour and blood is shed by each, the emotive, perceptual, social-psychological, and spiritual dimensions are core, not peripheral, concerns.[74]

Indeed, some aspects of peace-building are best understood by using religious approaches. The processes associated with reconciliation for instance – confession, repentance and forgiveness – are essentially religious rather than secular terms. They have arguably greater use when employed by religious rather than secular figures.[75] There are clear moral and political reasons why churches and governments should continue to invest in alternative methods of conflict resolution. The dilemma for many Christians arises when non-violent approaches appear to fail. Some Christian bodies, like the Quakers, see any form of violence as contrary to the mind of Christ. Others, too, have theological objections to any movement from non-violent to violent methods of conflict resolution.

There are interesting parallels between the way churches and states have reacted to theological or political attempts to prohibit war as a tool of statecraft. In 1928, states negotiated the Kellog-Briand Pact. This treaty committed its signatories not to use war as an instrument of national policy. These were the same signatory states which 11 years later fought in the Second World War. As the diplomatic historian Thomas Bailey observed, this treaty 'proved a monument to illusion. It was not only elusive but dangerous for it lulled the public into a false sense of security.'[76] The drafting of the Kellogg-Briand Pact reveals that states sought to include so many caveats and provisions in the treaty as to make it virtually meaningless. The Kellogg-Briand Pact testifies to the folly of drafting highly convoluted legal texts which fail to recognize or correspond with the actual feelings and demands of state practice. Any international treaty must reflect the underlying dynamics of power, culture and security, as well as the way states actually behave, otherwise it risks becoming a list of rules which are clear on paper but irrelevant to the real world.

These risks became apparent in July 1979 when the Church of England's General Synod debated a report, *Christians in a Violent World*. This report studied a number of issues relating to defence and disarmament, taking into account the 1978 Lambeth Conference resolution, which reiterated earlier conference declarations that 'war as a method of settling international disputes is incompatible with the teaching and example of Our Lord Jesus Christ'. The report submitted to the General Synod acknowledged the contribution of the Christian pacifist tradition but argued that 'most Christians would today, albeit with reluctance, reject this pacifist view as ideal and inapplicable to the actual contingencies of the real world'. By taking this stance the Church recognized that governments must provide for the security of their people, and the salient lesson of the causes of the two world wars was the need to apply 'the complicated and exacting doctrine of deterrence'.[77]

Noble though pacifism is, relying solely on non-violent conflict resolution can sometimes appear to run counter to the demands of common sense. It has repeatedly been labelled as morally and politically irresponsible, and compared to the policy of appeasement of the 1930s.[78] Contrary to Wink's thesis, history suggests pacifism 'does not offer readily applicable policy advice to public officials on matters of war and peace'. Instead 'it typically stresses the need for conversion in order to enable persons and communities to live non-violently, defencelessly, and is most pessimistic about the prospects of peace in a world that does not know Christ'.[79]

The theological and political limitations of Christian pacifism

Christian pacifism is open to a number of theological objections, which limit its political utility. It seems to assume that Jesus rejected the Old Testament. Yet Jesus recognized that Hebrew Scripture possesses divine authority, even if he sought to transform it. In particular he challenged the Pharisaic interpretation of Scripture as over-restrictive. Jesus never actually condemns the institution of war. On the contrary he converses with a Roman soldier and does not condemn him (Luke 7.4–9).[80]

This biblical ambiguity raises questions as to the context in which Jesus delivered the Sermon on the Mount. New Testament scholars generally agree that the Sermon on the Mount is better seen as a collection of Jesus' teachings that had been compiled from memory by his disciples than as a verbatim transcript of any single sermon.[81] Although the context in which Jesus delivered these teachings remains in doubt, it seems more likely that the sequence of sayings gathered together as the Sermon on the Mount fell – in Niebuhr's terms – within the private rather than the public sphere of attitudes and actions. It cannot be assumed Jesus' command to turn the other cheek meant that nations should remain passive when faced with invasion.

This is in no way to downplay the significance of Jesus' teachings.

Christian pacifism as a form of Christian perfectionism has a legitimate role within the churches, and within wider society. It upholds an absolute standard of human behaviour against which the compromises that politics necessitates can be judged. But, as a political strategy, it has serious limitations. This may explain why perfectionist groups, like the Mennonites, have traditionally eschewed the political sphere and refused to promote pacifism as a political strategy.

There is a significant distinction between those who attempt to live their lives prophetically according to such perfectionist principles and those who seek to interpret Jesus' teachings as a form of social ethics. Jesus' ethics relate to the individual person and not to the corporate or body politic. To argue that non-violent resistance offers a coherent political programme is a highly specific interpretation of the teachings from which such pacifist programmes draw their legitimacy.

Even acts of non-violent resistance can have negative consequences, as illustrated by the suffering of Lancashire cotton workers following Gandhi's promotion of the Indian boycott of English cotton. Morally, there may be no qualitative distinction between violent and some non-violent acts of resistance since both represent a breach of agape. Indeed, much of Gandhi's non-violent strategy was politically effective precisely because it had harmful effects. On this argument the differences between violent and non-violent acts of resistance are pragmatic rather than essential, since both accept the principle of coercion.

> The social consequences of the two methods are different, but the differences are in degree rather than in kind. Both place restraint upon liberty and both may destroy life and principle. Once the principle of coercion and resistance has been accepted as necessary to the social struggle and pure pacifism has thus been abandoned, the differences between violence and non-violence lose some of their significance though they remain important.[82]

To argue that non-violent resistance is morally more acceptable than war, and that it offers the best chance of securing harmonious relationships between parties, can lead to a prohibition of war under any circumstance. In some instances war can be preferable to surrender or living with the consequences of a tyrannical oppressor.

If Christian realism is too pessimistic about human nature then pacifism may also take too optimistic a view of human nature and human history. Pacifism reflects an ideal of human nature, which fails to take the fall seriously.[83] To adopt such an ideal image of human beings is to fail to recognize the human capacity to do ill. To assume that such evil can be resisted through aggressive acts of good will can, at times, both underestimate the nature of such threats and overplay the effectiveness of Christian pacifism to manage such threats. A theology, like Christian pacifism, which appears to be built so squarely on biblical revelation and subject to little historical rational or experiential validation, can appear at times politically irresponsible and morally confused.

Conclusion

This chapter started by asking questions about the authority by which churches contribute to public policy discussions on war and peace. It is clear that as far as this issue is concerned there is little within the Bible that could be seen as providing clear, explicit and unambiguous moral teaching. We have argued, too, that there are limitations either in adopting a literal approach to the Bible or in looking to Scripture for easy answers on contemporary issues. Such approaches tend to be highly selective in their use of Scripture and generally ignore the conflicting statements that the Bible generates on a range of issues.

Literal interpretations of the Bible that give rise to either a dogmatic militarism or pacifism tend to falsify Scripture by seeing it as amounting to a set of timeless instructions rather than as a set of historical documents reflecting the age in which it was written. Rather than seeing the Bible as the word of God revealed, many have come to see that when the Bible is seen as a whole and in its historical context it cannot be used as an unmediated source of systematic teaching on contemporary issues. This underlines the importance of reason, a God-given gift which is needed to give the Bible any contemporary relevance. As John Macquarrie writes:

> If the demand for relevance and intelligibility is to be met, then there will always be a danger of infringing the autonomous – and even judgmental – character of the primordial revelation; but this must be weighed against the other

danger of so insulating the revelation against all contact with the changing forms of secular culture, that it becomes encapsulated, and shut off from everything else in life.[84]

The Bible requires a constant effort of interpretation if it is to have any resonance inside and outside the churches. Churches and their moral theologians have a responsibility to offer public guidance on how such interpretations might usefully occur.

The danger is that reasoning requires value judgements to be made as to whether a certain act is right or wrong. This reasoning will change as human developments continue to progress. This in turn raises the question: 'Where is the authority which can continue to invest this form of reasoning with cogency?'[85] One such explanation is provided by the preamble to those briefing papers and reports previously produced by the Church of England's Board for Social Responsibility:

> The Church is asked to comment and make moral judgements on many issues. In responding to such requests the Church encourages its members to draw on the resources of Scripture, Tradition, and Reason to enable them to engage, prayerfully and intelligently, with the matter under debate. It is neither surprising nor reprehensible that Christians will, in good faith, reach different conclusions on particular issues. The Board for Social Responsibility's Briefing Papers are provided as resources to enable Christians to think through difficult moral issues for themselves.

The combination of Scripture, tradition and reason escapes the dilemma of relying solely on any one source of authority. While reason gives renewed meaning to Scripture it also gives rise to tradition. While reason is needed to challenge and to question a priori assumptions it has to be exercised in creative tension with Scripture and tradition.

This approach has parallels with how some member states of the United Nations have started to interpret the UN Charter. If member states abided solely by the letter rather than the spirit of the Charter then interventions to prevent or stop such moral outrages as occurred in Kosovo would have been impossible. The Charter after all prohibits the interference in the internal affairs of another nation state. To have adhered strictly to the Charter would have meant standing helplessly by as innocents were slaughtered, as was the case in Rwanda. This would have turned the Charter on its head so damaging the UN's credibility and authority. Instead, some member states justified their action by drawing on customary case law, which legitimized similar interventions as in Somalia. The political reasoning behind the decision to intervene in Kosovo was therefore done in conjunction with, rather than in isolation from, the Charter and the substantial body of customary case law that it has generated. This reasoning was not however universally shared by all members of the United Nations Security Council who argued that a literal reading of the Charter prohibited such interventions.

How then have Scripture, tradition and reason influenced the churches' understanding of war and peace? Since wars have been an unfortunate but inevitable part of history, there have been plenty of opportunities for churches to develop their own tradition and understanding as to whether a particular use of force could be considered morally acceptable or desirable. The churches' thinking has in turn been challenged and refined by those instances where human relations have broken down and where countries find themselves at war. The methodology employed has been that body of social teaching commonly associated with the just war tradition. This tradition was developed by St Augustine, refined by St Aquinas and reworked by Hugo Grotius.

The just war tradition provides clear rules, principles and values which have wide appeal and validity and from which a particular judgement may be deduced as to the morality of any use of force. The great strength of this approach is that it is rational and requires a movement from the general to the particular. The danger however is that the greater this movement, the more likely there is to be controversy and disagreement as to the interpretation or application of the principles governing the tradition. This disagreement is likely to be heightened if there is a dispute about the empirical facts that comprise any particular case. The following chapter explores this just war tradition in greater detail.

3 | Rediscovering the Just War Tradition

Though I do not accept the validity of the just war tradition as a source of moral guidance, I feel obliged to play the rhetorical game . . . it is a game. Were the conditions of the just war ever honestly applied to an actual war, they would lead to behavioural conclusions identical to those required by the pacifism to which I personally subscribe.

(Gordon Zahn[1])

The just war tradition has its roots both in natural law and Christian theology and has been developed through a continuing dialogue between secular and religious sources. The interaction between diverse and competing actors, including theologians, military commanders and politicians, means that the just war tradition cannot be reduced to a set of moral assumptions or ideals. Participants within this dialogue have sought to shape and develop the tradition so that its relevance is retained even when it is applied to entirely new security challenges. This dialogue has shaped policy-making decisions on war by rules governing the conduct of war, while continuing to inform the consciences of individuals grappling with the ethical dilemmas of war.

Some moral theorists like James Turner Johnston see the just war tradition 'as a body of moral wisdom deeply and broadly rooted in Western ideals, institutions and experiences'.[2] Paul Ramsey sees it as inherent in the idea of good politics itself, arising out of some form of common moral wisdom of humankind rather than any particular Christian tradition.[3] For Michael Walzer, the tradition represents a set of ideas, which have been shaped out of the human experience of war.[4] For others the value of the just war theory lies in 'sustaining and developing a moral culture of war that encourages its more limited use and conduct', which might 'perhaps lead to the ostracism of states that ignore moral constraints'.[5] Most pacifists argue, however, that it amounts to nothing more 'than a means by which Christians have been able to salve their consciences when taking part in war, a compromise between a theoretically non-violent Christianity and the practical imperatives imposed by civic loyalties'.[6]

From the perspective of the institutional churches, the tradition's value lies in its ability to set out an ethical framework which enables churches to contribute to discussions on war in a way that ensures that they are heard. The nurturing of such an approach becomes particularly important in a secular age, in which churches often find themselves speaking from the margins and in a language which tends to make assumptions about common moral values which are increasingly difficult to sustain in an individualistic and 'privatized' society. It is perhaps surprising that in a secular age where serious religious language has been marginalized Britain still retains a public theology on war and peace. But this makes it all the more important to clarify the precise meaning of the terms used in just war discourse.

This chapter examines the origins and developments of the just war tradition, and how it has determined the rules of war, both in terms of a particular decision to go to war and the rules of engagement to be followed once war has begun. Particular attention is paid to those threats that have emerged since the end of the Cold War that challenge the way states have traditionally viewed and used force. The rise of intra-state violence, ethnic conflict and terrorism requires creative international responses. The trend towards humanitarian intervention and pre-emptive military action suggest that in the West at least the nature of warfare has now radically changed. States are now more likely to use force to punish evil and to intervene on the side of the oppressed. Since 1989 the use of force has increasingly taken the form of quasi-police action.

These developments have led some commentators to question the continued relevance of the just war tradition as a guide to morally legitimate action. This chapter argues that just war thinking can still assist reflection on the ethical implications of these developments. Many of the current security threats vexed the minds of early just war scholars. While the sovereign state system still remains the dominant pattern in the international system, it is possible to discern a pattern of cross-cutting communities and governance that bears some resemblance to the situation as it existed before the Peace of Westphalia in 1648. Recalling how scholars approached these issues before that time might provide a helpful contribution to the post-Cold War debate as to when it is legitimate to use force in the pursuit of justice.

The origins of the just war theory

When St Augustine of Hippo wrote *The City of God*, he was writing at a time of early Christian history when Christian communities lived in relative isolation from mainstream society.[7] The evidence from Tertullian and Origen writing in the third century is that, for the most part, Christians viewed the shedding of blood as unlawful. They believed prayer was the appropriate Christian response to injustice.[8] These early Christian attitudes to war changed with the Edict of Milan (AD 313) and Constantine's conversion to Christianity. Christians were no longer a persecuted minority, but instead they occupied positions of authority and influence in society. Their views were sought on a range of issues. To decline all participation in politics would have been seen as undermining confidence in the Empire. Yet such participation involved a challenge to existing Christian assumptions and the articulation of a new understanding of the emerging relationship between Church and Empire. It also required a challenge to prevailing Roman prejudices, which tended to view Christianity as a parochial religion incapable of making sense of world history.[9] According to Peter Bathory, Augustine's task was not an 'escape from the world, but a start at living more freely within it'.[10]

Augustine moved beyond Tertullian and Origen in holding that war, as such, should not be categorically rejected or condoned.[11] To Augustine war can be morally justifiable, because in parts of the Old Testament God is seen to command it. By interpreting Jesus' actions and commands in a way that was complementary rather than contradictory to the Old Testament, Augustine developed a coherent Christian approach to war.[12]

War is a lamentable consequence of sin. While the use of force in self-defence is forbidden by Jesus' command that we love our neighbour, this same command obliges Christians to act as the 'Good Samaritan'. While original sin taints all human action, including war, to the extent that it cannot be judged moral, there are circumstances in which war might be the lesser of two evils. These would be legitimate circumstances in which war may be justified even if it cannot be fully legitimate morally.[13]

St Augustine's genius and probably his greatest gift to Christian political theology was his ability to reconcile a non-Christian theory of civil society with the promise of the New Testament. By urging the early Church to distinguish between the Church in the earthly and the heavenly city, he encouraged it to engage with and challenge all that is corruptible and imperfect in a fallen world. The result was to turn Christianity from a relatively exclusive sect, with strict rules of membership with little feel or responsibility for society or government, into an inclusive Church, with responsibility for providing moral guidance to both society and government on contentious issues like the ethics of war.

Understanding the just war tradition

The shift in general political philosophy achieved by Augustine allowed Christians to participate in the development of the just war tradition. In its simplest form just war theory argues that certain conditions and criteria need to be met before any military action occurs. It has two thematic branches, classically denoted by the terms *jus ad bellum* and *jus in bello*. *Jus ad bellum* consists of seven principles, which need to be met to justify the resort to war. These include that war must have a *just cause*, be waged by a *proper authority* and with a *right intention*, be undertaken only if there is *reasonable chance of success* and if the total good outweighs the total evil expected (i.e. overall *proportionality*). It must also be used as a *last resort* and be waged for the end of peace. Complementing these principles are those relating to the conduct of war, *jus in bello*, which focuses on two concerns: *discrimination* – the avoidance of intentional harm to non-combatants – and *proportionality of means* – the requirement that only such force be employed as is strictly necessary to secure one's objective. Although these principles constitute what is commonly known as the just war theory, they do not, in themselves, define a just war. Before that can be done it will be helpful to examine the historical background and particular meaning of each of the criteria.

Just cause

Central to any understanding of the just war theory is the question of just cause. Aquinas quotes Augustine when he says:

We usually describe the just war as one that avenges wrong, that is, when a nation or state has to be punished for refusing either to make amends for outrages done by its subjects or to restore what it has seized injuriously.

Aquinas argued that the sword could only be taken up against those 'who deserve it on account of some fault'. It is clear from these grounds that just cause can be found where there is what amounts to aggression which, as Michael Walzer suggests, reflects a 'singular and undifferentiated crime, because, in all its forms, it challenges rights that are worth dying for'.[14] Aquinas did not restrict his meaning of 'justness' to wars of self-defence, but allowed for what would now be termed anticipatory self-defence. He did not imply that it would be right to take pre-emptive action without provocation; rather Aquinas restricted its use to a form of self-defence when attack appeared to be imminent.

Hugo Grotius' *De Jure Belli ac Pacis*, written in 1623, towards the end of the Thirty-Years War, refined the boundaries of what constituted just cause.[15] Just cause was thereafter taken to mean the right to self-defence. The inherited categories of punishment and the recovery of something injuriously taken were subsumed within a broader definition of the right to self-defence. His aim was to distinguish between wars of self-interest and those motivated by justice. In this way it became easier to make objective judgements as to the morality of any war, which were not dependent upon the sovereign's subjective judgements.

The danger with subjective judgements is that it is almost always the case that each side in a conflict believes in the justness of its cause. Objective judgements are less arbitrary since they require 'a more sober and even more sceptical assessment of one's own claim to justice', which leads 'perhaps to a more modest or economical formulation' of just cause.[16] Objectivity can lead, however, to a sense of moral certitude, which can spill over into crusading self-righteousness. As a result, just war theory requires an examination of the ruler's motives. This scrutiny highlights the ruler's own moral fallibility and even responsibility for the war, which prevents any moral triumphalism.

The tension between subjective and objective reasoning contributed to the codification of what now constitutes 'just cause' within international law. The UN's original raison d'être was 'to save the succeeding generations from the scourge of war, which twice in our lifetime has brought untold sorrow to mankind'. Article 2(4) outlaws interstate war:

> All members shall refrain in their international relations from the threat or use of force against the territorial integrity or political independence of any state, or in any other manner inconsistent with the Purposes of the United Nations.

A strict reading of the UN Charter provides only two legal exemptions to the ban on the 'the threat or use of force': action in response to a perceived threat and acts of self-defence.

Article 39 of the Charter authorizes collective action with respect to peace, breaches of the peace and acts of aggression. The type of action envisaged by the UN is set out in Articles 41–43. While Article 41 concerns collective action not entailing the use of arms, Article 43 legitimates 'such action by air, sea, or land forces as may be necessary to maintain or restore international peace and security'. From a just war perspective it is significant that non-military action precedes military action, so underlining the point that all non-military options need to be reasonably pursued before military action can be taken.

Legitimate authority

The second just war requirement is legitimate authority. The feudal system of medieval society made this especially important. Early just war theory located the authority to make war with the sovereign. Private persons had no right to redress their grievances through the use of arms. The privatization of war was therefore prohibited. Hugo Grotius refined the just war deliberations on lawful authority by transferring sovereignty from the ruler of a political entity to the entity itself.[17] Grotius anticipated the emergence of the Treaty of Westphalia and with it the modern state system. Thereafter the justification for going to war was presented in legal rather than moral terms.[18] The interests of the state were to be seen as separate from the interests of the sovereign. This development reflected the desire to escape the religiously motivated wars that had torn Europe apart after the Reformation.

The question of legitimate authority remains a contested issue within contemporary just war debates and within international politics. It provides one of the main areas of disagreement between idealists, who hanker after some form of world government, and realists, who insist that the nation state remains sovereign. Some argue that authorization for military action rests with the United Nations, while others see this right still resting with nation states. Article 51 recognizes this dilemma:

> Nothing in the present Charter shall impair the inherent right of individual or collective self-defence if an armed attack occurs against a member of the United Nations, until the Security Council has taken measures necessary to maintain international peace and security.

The mechanism by which UN members contribute to a Security Council action, as prescribed by Articles 43–47, has rarely been exercised. This would appear to support John Finnis' argument:

> Although a world government can now be envisaged as in some sense a practical possibility and although leaders and people ought to do what they responsibly can to bring such a world government into being, these considerations do not justify the conclusion that, in the meantime, states must behave precisely as if they already had a common superior, effectively responsible for maintaining the world wide common good, on whom they must treat the police power as having being devolved.[19]

The Security Council has only authorized force on two occasions: against Korea (1950–53) and against Iraq (1990–91).[20] This has not prevented the UN from mandating various peacekeeping operations such as those in Kosovo, East Timor and the Congo. But these peace-keeping operations are dependent on member states volunteering their military services. If the Security Council requests military assistance then each member state decides according to its own constitutional process whether or not it is right to participate. While the Security Council might therefore decide that just cause exists, the legal authority for authorizing military action rests not with the Security Council but with individual member states.

Ultimately the legitimacy of any governmental action rests on a broad public consensus. While the US President has authority to commit US troops abroad, this is usually done with the approval of Congress. The limitation of the President's constitutional power to authorize war is a recent development. The experiences of Vietnam where successive US Presidents committed troops to Vietnam, without congressional approval, led to the 1973 War Powers Act. Although subsequent Presidents have argued that this resolution unconstitutionally infringes the President's power as Commander-in-Chief, and while the Supreme Court has never ruled on this issue, no US President has ignored this Act. Regardless of whether the UN mandated member states to commit forces to military action under Article 42, domestic procedures still need to be followed to ensure that any military action is properly authorized and legitimate.

Right intent

Aquinas believed that lawful authority and just cause were necessary but not sufficient conditions to wage a just war. The motives influencing the decision to wage war needed close scrutiny. This criterion has both negative and positive implications. Put negatively by St Augustine it entails: 'The passion for inflicting harm, the cruel thirst for vengeance, an unpacific and relentless spirit, the fever of revolt, the lust of power, and such like things, all these are rightly condemned in war.' Put positively by St Augustine it meant: 'True religion looks upon as peaceful those wars that are waged not for motives of aggrandisement or cruelty, but with the object of securing peace, of punishing evil doers, and of uplifting the good.' In other words, those who wage war must intend to promote a good and to avoid a greater evil. While there is no equivalent of right intent within contemporary law, the question of hidden or undisclosed motives remains an essential part of modern political inquiry. This is especially so since many belligerents use 'just cause' in a rhetorical fashion to hide ulterior aims.

While just cause and legitimate authority are objective criteria, right intent concerns the subjective intentions of those who wage war. Regan notes:

> War decision-makers have right intention if – and only if – they aim to conform their decisions to the objective criteria of just war. In other words, statesmen are just warriors if – and only if – they strive to reason rightly about war and warfare, and act accordingly.[21]

Right intent cannot be isolated from other just war criteria. A statesman who wages war must show that he has sought to avoid war, has the authority to do so, and that the war is waged for limited objectives. Similarly statesmen should ensure that their conduct of the war conforms to the principles of just war in that there should be no intentional attacks on civilian populations or use of force which is disproportionate to the cause for which the war is being fought. The intent therefore in waging war must at all times be the restoration of peace, rather than any quest for territorial or self-enrichment.

Reasonable chance of success, last resort and proportionality

Before a war can be judged to be just in the *jus ad bellum* tradition the criteria relating to reasonable chance of success, last resort and overall proportionality must also be satisfied. 'Reasonable chance of success' involves statesmen and their military commanders making a prudential calculation as to the likelihood that the means used will secure the desired end. 'Proportionality of ends' requires calculations to be made as to whether the overall good to be achieved is greater than any damage that will be inflicted in achieving it. 'Last resort' stipulates that alternative means to securing the desired objective must, within reason, be pursued before any decision is taken to use force.

These criteria involve the assessment of subjective factors. Assessing proportionality involves a speculative judgement as to the worth of the cause and whether that cause justifies the loss of life.[22] This involves hypothetical projections as to the war's likely course and an estimate of the casualties that might be incurred as a result of military action. For a war to be proportionate these projections need to be set against the value of the intended war aim. As Regan observes:

> Despite the indemonstrable values and the factual uncertainties involved, it is the function of practical reason to make such judgements, and statesmen need to make these judgements if they are to ascertain that they have a proportionate just cause to wage war.[23]

Reasoning that requires subjective judgements is always open to miscalculation. Some experts might disagree with the statesmen's reasoning. This uncertainty does not itself render any subsequent

military action illegitimate. Just war theory does not require statesmen to quantify the unquantifiable. Instead, 'the question of proportion must be evaluated . . . from the viewpoint of the hierarchy
of strictly moral values', which recognizes that 'there are greater
evils than the physical death and destruction wrought in war'.[24]

Similar disagreements occur over the question of last resort. Last
resort requires a government to make a judgement that all *reasonable*
efforts at peacefully resolving a dispute have been tried. In situations
where a country finds itself under attack a government's only option
might be to rely on military force as means of defence. In other
circumstances, however, alternative methods of conflict resolution
might be explored. In this respect last resort requires a serious and
genuine commitment to peacemaking.

As with other just war criteria the question of last resort should
not be interpreted too narrowly. Weigel remarks:

> Among those who have forgotten the just war tradition, while
> retaining its language, the classic *ad bellum* criteria of 'last
> resort' is usually understood in simplistically mathematical
> terms. The use of proportionate and discriminate force is the
> last point in a series of options, and prior, non-military options
> (legal, diplomatic, and economic) must be serially exhausted
> before the criterion of last resort is satisfied. This is both an
> excessively mechanistic understanding of last resort and a
> prescription for danger.[25]

It is always possible to imagine one more peace conference or
another round of shuttle diplomacy to resolve a crisis. Just war
theory requires only that all reasonable efforts have been taken.
There is little value in entering into a negotiation with an aggressor
state if that state aims to use the negotiations as means of cementing
territorial acquisitions. This would be to devalue the justness of a
state's cause. As Coates recognizes: 'Here as elsewhere, moral considerations go hand in hand with political and military ones, and the
moral judgement needs to be informed by a certain realism.'[26]

The subjective nature of these criteria has led some to question
their relevance. James Turner Johnston argues that while they are
derived historically from Roman practice, 'international law does
not address them specifically, and religious just war theorists have
paid little attention to them historically'.[27] It is evident however

that these criteria have found resonance with the wider public. Some contemporary critiques of the ethics of a particular use of force appear to downplay the justness of a particular cause, preferring instead to question whether or not all diplomatic and economic alternatives have been exhausted.[28]

Paul Ramsey has described this logic as amounting to a form of just war pacifism. The destructiveness of modern warfare is judged to be so serious that war can never be a last resort for serving justice and peace.[29] The consequence is to turn the just war logic on its head.[30]

> Since at least everyone seeks peace and desires justice, the ends for which war may be fought are not nearly so important in the theory of just war as is the moral and political wisdom contained in its reflection upon the conduct or means of a war.[31]

This interpretation of the just war tradition runs the risk of reducing the tradition to a morality of means. Maintaining the integrity of the just war tradition requires a more holistic and balanced approach.

During the Cold War the potential for nuclear confrontation between the great powers led some ethicists to argue that the threat of an apocalyptic war made war immoral. The end of the Cold War has lessened this threat. Similarly, developments in military technology have led military and political pundits to argue that responsible warfare is now a distinct possibility.[32] This does not mean warfare is casualty free, but it does suggest that there is greater chance that the harm done might not outweigh the good achieved.[33] Conflict in the post-Cold War era resembles conventional rather than nuclear models of warfare. This shift has seen the 'partial moral rehabilitation of armed force' as an instrument of statecraft.[34]

Jus in bello

The *jus in bello* tradition consists of two elements: discrimination and proportionality of means. Discrimination demands that every effort should be made to avoid direct or intentional harm to non-combatants. Proportionality of means requires military commanders to avoid needless destruction when pursuing justified ends. In theory the *jus in bello* dimension of just war only has relevance once the decision has been taken that the *jus ad bellum* criteria have been met. In reality there has been a growing practice to prioritize *jus in bello* over *jus ad bellum* considerations. Weigel observes:

> Its effect in moral analysis is to turn the tradition inside out, such that war-conduct (*in bello*) questions of proportionality and discrimination take theological precedence over what were traditionally assumed to be prior war decision (*ad bellum*) questions. This inversion is theologically problematic because it places the heaviest burden of moral analysis on what are inevitably contingent judgements. In the nature of the case, we can have less surety about *in bello* proportion and discrimination than we can about the *ad bellum* questions. The tradition logically starts with *ad bellum* questions because the just war tradition is a tradition of statecraft: a tradition that attempts to define morally worthy political ends.[35]

This trend reflects the destructiveness of nineteenth- and twentieth-century warfare. The end of the Cold War and with it the threat of a nuclear holocaust, allied to the increasing sophistication of military software as illustrated in both Gulf Wars, suggests it is necessary to rediscover the classic just war tradition.

Classically understood, the just war understanding of both proportionality and discrimination aims to ensure that moral reasoning is not lost in the fog of war. Proportionality requires that the use of force is neither gratuitous nor excessive. The legitimate use of force is dependent on combatants mustering only as much force as is necessary to secure the legitimate political objective of any military campaign. Discrimination holds that military force should only be directed against those directly involved in a war effort.

In both instances, just war theory requires a moral analysis that is informed by an awareness of the military and political realities of war. In doing so, the just war tradition prescribes a basic respect for life, which seeks to ensure that the act of war itself does not dehumanize either those engaged in war or those who run the risk of being caught in its wake. It recalls the story of the Good Samaritan and reformulates the question 'Who is my neighbour?' to 'Who is my enemy?' How can the love for one's enemy, and the recognition that enemies never stop being human, be preserved in war? These questions highlight what Niditch describes as 'a conflict within each of us between compassion and enmity'.[36]

Two writers, Francisco de Vitoria and Hugo Grotius, informed these *jus ad bellum* arguments.[37] Vitoria argued that soldiers have not only a right but also an obligation to refuse to fight in a war they consider unjust or a war leading to the intentional killing of innocent civilians. However, he maintained that in some circumstances the foreseen killing of innocents, as in a siege, is legitimate and necessary if it leads to justice and the restoration of peace. This concession rests on the basis that states must ensure that greater evil does not arise through permitting actions which would be averted by the war.

Hugo Grotius explored further the predicament exposed by Vitoria. His definition of the 'innocent' is taken to include women, children and the elderly, as well as those whose manner of life is opposed to war, such as farmers and artisans. He followed Aquinas in accepting the principle of double effect, believing that careful consideration needs to be given to the intended consequences of any action. He urged restraint in all circumstances unless 'the good which our action has in view is much greater than the evil which is feared, or unless the good and evil balance'. This seemingly contradictory position which prohibits the killing of innocents on the one hand but allows it in others has been at the centre of many subsequent debates about the ethics governing military engagement.

Neither Vitoria nor Grotius could have predicted nineteenth- and twentieth-century developments where states claimed for themselves the right to go to war or the means with which wars were fought. The indiscriminate nature of warfare in the nineteenth century led to efforts to enshrine the principles of non-combatant immunity and proportionality of means in international law. The Geneva Convention and the Hague Conventions now provide the basis of international law and regulations governing those conditions which might arise in war.

The Hague Conventions of 1899 and 1907 were primarily concerned with the rights and duties of belligerents. They prohibit both the killing and wounding of soldiers who surrender, as well as the destruction of an opponent's property unless 'imperatively demanded by the necessity of war'.[38] They forbid attacks on undefended civilian dwellings and stipulate the steps that need to be taken to protect places of cultural, civic and religious value. The Conventions hold the occupying powers responsible for maintaining law and order but they prohibit the imposition of general penalties on account of actions by individuals.

In contrast, the Geneva Convention provides protection and treatment of those non-combatants not party to a conflict. This covers sick and wounded combatants, prisoners of war and civilians held by a foreign power. Its binding principles are that persons who unwittingly find themselves caught up in a conflict or those taking no part in the war should be spared and be treated humanely. The wounded, the sick and all medical resources were to be respected under the sign of the Red Cross or Red Crescent. Similarly, prisoners of war must be treated humanely and the names given to the International Committee of the Red Cross who have the right of access to check on their condition. Civilians are to be allowed to live normal lives so far as circumstances permit. This prohibits deportations, pillage and the indiscriminate destruction of property during war.[39]

Additional Protocols to the Geneva Convention agreed in 1977 set out the basic principle that acts of war which cause wanton and unnecessary damage and suffering should be avoided. Wanton damage also extended to 'widespread, long term and severe damage to the environment'. Everything possible has to be done to avoid harming civilians and to ensure that incidental damage is not excessive in relation to the 'concrete and direct military advantage'. The Protocols extend the Convention's scope to cover liberation struggles and internal conflicts against dissident armed forces.[40]

These international conventions provide a codification of the ethics of war conduct. They prescribe certain standards of behaviour which states are obliged to follow during a war's prosecution. While these conventions cannot remove what Nietzsche called 'war's true ugliness', they have gone some way to humanizing war. For war to be just, it now has to be humane. Some have argued that this amounts to a regrounding of war on humanistic foundations, which removes any philosophical or moral defence of cruelty.[41] This limited concept of war stands in contrast, however, to the rather more comprehensive ideologies of violence and enmity that have marked recent conflicts in Rwanda, Bosnia, Kosovo, Sierre Leone and Liberia. The failure to see the humanity of one's enemy also accounts for the terrorist activities of Al Qaeda, ETA, the IRA and Hamas. The idea of restraint in war is therefore by no means universally accepted.[42]

The new security agenda

Since the end of the Cold War the prohibition of the threat or use of force as enshrined within the UN Charter has become the point of heated disagreement between UN member states. The emergence of new security challenges (terrorism, intra-state conflict, humanitarian disasters and rogue regimes) has led some states to reinterpret the right to self-defence as contained within Article 51 in a manner possibly at odds with the meaning intended by the Charter's original signatories. At the same time the unilateralization of multilateral decision-making through the delegation of UN peacekeeping, as authorized under Chapter VII of the UN Charter, to regional organizations such as NATO has reduced the UN's role to a formal rather than substantive one in upholding international peace and security. States' adherence to international law and to the UN Charter has become increasingly unpredictable.

These developments, both in terms of new security challenges and state practice, raise questions that challenge traditional understandings of when it is right and proper to use military force. It is clear that the UN founding fathers had inter-state conflict in mind when they sought to prohibit the use of force. Inter-state war has proved, however, to be the exception rather than the norm. Civil wars, ethnic conflict, cross-border guerrilla incursions and limited inter-state fighting have been more common than fully blown inter-state war. The end of the Cold War, and with it the emergence of the USA as the sole remaining superpower, has led to a more flexible interpretation of the Charter. The discernible trend is for states to use force to promote democracy, restore order in failed states, protect their citizens overseas and as a means to combat terrorism.

During the Cold War the UK and the USA were opposed to any broadening of the interpretation of Article 2(4), out of fear that it would benefit the USSR. Since 1989 these same countries have pressed for an open and dynamic interpretation of the UN Charter. Russia, China and many Middle Eastern countries, as well as those countries within what was previously considered the Non-Aligned Movement, remain committed to a minimalist reading of the Charter. This lack of international consensus has created ambiguity in practice, which points to the growing ineffectiveness of international law in conditioning state behaviour.

Just intervention

One of the most notable developments since the end of the Cold War has been the trend towards intervention in the internal affairs of another nation state without UN sanction. The question of whether this practice is legal would appear at first glance unequivocal. The Charter clearly prohibits the use of force except in cases of self-defence and where action has been authorized by the Security Council. The Charter prohibits the interference in the internal affairs of another state. And yet there have been a number of examples, such as NATO's action in Kosovo, where states have assumed this right for themselves.

Humanitarian interventions are not merely a post-Cold War phenomenon. India's intervention in 1971 to secure Bangladeshi independence from Pakistan, Tanzania's removal of Idi Amin from Uganda in 1978, and the Vietnamese overthrow of Pol Pot in Cambodia in 1978 could all be classed as humanitarian interventions.[13] Significantly, however, all countries involved justified their action on the ground of self-defence, rather than invoking some doctrine of humanitarian intervention. While their actions avoided Security Council condemnation, France and the UK made clear that human rights violations could not justify the use of force.

In 1982 the Foreign and Commonwealth Office cautioned against developing a doctrine of humanitarian intervention on the grounds that humanitarian motives were always intertwined with other motives and because the benefits of humanitarian intervention had never previously been used as justification for intervention. Consequently, it argued that 'the best case that can be made in support of humanitarian intervention is that it cannot be said to be unambiguously illegal'.[44] By 1992 the Foreign and Commonwealth Office's position had altered:

> We believe that international intervention without the invitation of the country concerned can be justified in cases of extreme humanitarian need. This is why we were prepared to commit British forces to Operation Haven, mounted by the coalition in response to the refugee crisis involving the Iraqi Kurds. The deployment of these forces was entirely consistent with the objectives of SCR 688.[45]

It is difficult to see how what had been 'not unambiguously illegal' in 1982 had somehow become legal in 1992. The end of the Cold war and the demise of the USSR allowed for political revisions in the interpretation of the UN Charter so reflecting the new power configurations.

NATO's intervention in Kosovo revealed fundamental splits within the international community as to the legality of humanitarian intervention. Russia and China argued that NATO's action was a violation of the UN Charter and especially Article 4(2).[46] It was the responsibility of the UN Security Council to maintain international peace and security, and this authorization was necessary before regional organizations could take action under Chapter VII of the UN Charter. The UN Secretary General appeared to agree with this argument by reminding NATO of the Security Council's primary responsibility in matters regarding peace and security.

Those defending NATO's action offered a number of legal justifications. France, the UK and the USA argued that while the Security Council had not explicitly authorized the use of force, Serbia's failure to meet its responsibilities under three UN Security Council resolutions provided implicit authority for military action.[47] Rather than invoking the general right of humanitarian intervention these states argued in favour of some doctrine of implied authorization by the UN Security Council.[48] Slovenia and Belgium argued, however, that UN humanitarian action in Yugoslavia and Somalia and the work done by regional organizations on behalf of the UN in Liberia and Sierre Leone showed the existence of a general doctrine of humanitarian intervention.[49]

Yugoslavia brought legal action against 10 of the 19 NATO member states following the war. In its ruling the International Court of Justice expressed concern as to the war's legality, but it declined to make a formal ruling one way or the other. In the absence of a clear legal ruling some states have continued to develop the doctrine of humanitarian intervention.[50] These doctrinal developments occurred despite the continuing opposition of Russia, China, and Middle Eastern states, as well as India and Pakistan. Adopting UNSC resolution 1244 following a cessation of hostilities in Kosovo and agreement on the principles of a peace process mitigated criticisms of NATO's actions in Kosovo.

Anticipatory self-defence

A state's use of force to defend itself before its territory has even been attacked is legally and morally contentious. States have shied away from claiming anticipatory self-defence as the justification for military action. Instead, they have used a wider right to self-defence. The USA did not rely on anticipatory self-defence during the Cuban missile crisis of 1962 to justify the interception of USSR nuclear missiles; rather, it relied on regional peacekeeping under Chapter VIII of the UN Charter.[51] Israel claimed that pre-emptive strikes against Egypt, Jordan and Syria in 1967 were compatible with Article 51 on the grounds that the closure of the Straits of Tiran to Israel constituted an act of war. While Iraq initially defended its invasion of Iran in 1980 on the grounds of anticipatory self-defence, it later argued that its military action was in response to a prior attack by Iran.

While 'this reluctance expressly to use anticipatory self-defence is in itself a clear indication of the doubtful status of this justification for the use of force', there have been instances where states have invoked this doctrine in their defence.[52] In 1981 Israel attacked an Iraqi nuclear reactor on the grounds that the reactor was designed to produce nuclear bombs against Israel. In subsequent Security Council debates, Israel defended its position by arguing that anticipatory self-defence was legal, rather than relying on any clear precedent set in state practice.[53] In the discussions that followed, the USA argued that Israel's action was illegal because Israel had failed to exhaust peaceful means of resolving this dispute. The UK and France argued that the action was not justified because evidence previously presented by the International Energy and Atomic Agency showed Iraq was not planning to use the reactor for the development of nuclear weapons.[54] Russia and China contended that the principle of anticipatory self-defence was incompatible with Article 51.[55]

In 1999 the USA and the UK extended the rules of engagement governing the no-fly zones over Iraq to include anticipatory self-defence. Previously they had restricted their actions to self-defence, attacking only those missile sites posing a threat to allied aircraft. In 1999, however, they extended this remit to include any perceived threat to their aircraft such as command and control centres. They justified their actions on the grounds that such steps were necessary to ensure the safety of those patrolling the no-fly zones.[56] As with the Israeli attack of 1981 international criticism was varied. Russia and China argued that this was illegal because Britain and the United States were acting unilaterally without the expressed authorization of the UN.

These examples show that the concept of anticipatory self-defence has a controversial status under international law and within state practice. States prefer to build a stronger case for their actions by relying on an extended interpretation of armed attack rather than opening a doctrinal debate about the legitimacy and morality of anticipatory self-defence. States try to bring any action within the remit and scope of Article 51 rather than seeking to justify their actions by expressly arguing that there is a wider right to self-defence under customary international law.

Terrorism

States have also interpreted Article 51 widely to justify military responses to terrorist attacks or attacks on nationals abroad. The USA defended its actions in Afghanistan on the grounds of self-defence in the wake of the unprecedented attacks of 11 September 2001. There was no substantial international criticism of the USA's actions in Afghanistan. It is evident, however, from past incidents where states justified their counter-terrorist activity by reference to Article 51, that there is not international consensus as to the validity of such a legal interpretation.

In December 1968 Israel launched an aerial offensive on Beirut. This was in response to an earlier terrorist attack on an Israeli plane at Athens airport. Israel argued that Lebanon was complicit in the attack because it had permitted Arab terrorists to set up their headquarters in Beirut, so encouraging the terrorist attack. Although the Security Council unanimously condemned Israel's actions in UNSC resolution 262, the reasons given by some Security Council members suggest that there was a lack of agreement as to whether Israel's action contravened a principle of international law or whether the specific incident was wrong.[57] The USA accepted Israel's reasoning, but believed Israel's actions were wrong because Lebanon had not been responsible for the attack and because the response was not proportionate. Other Security Council members, including the UK, argued the act contravened an important principle of international law.[58]

The USA used similar reasoning to justify its actions in the 1980s and 1990s. In 1986 the USA bombed government targets in Tripoli, following terrorist attacks by Libya against US nationals living abroad. America reported its action to the Security Council and justified its position as one of self-defence under Article 51.[59] Most states rejected this claim arguing that the right to self-defence should be narrowly interpreted. The British Government, which had allowed the USA to use UK bases from which to fly their missions, supported the action, arguing that 'the right of self-defence is not an entirely passive right'.[60] The UK and France vetoed the resolution condemning US action.

In 1998, the USA responded to terrorist attacks on its embassies in Kenya and Ethiopia by attacking alleged terrorist training camps in Afghanistan and the Sudan. As in 1986 the USA argued that it was exercising its right to self-defence and sought by its action to deter further terrorist attacks. The military response was only taken once efforts to convince Sudan and Afghanistan to close down the terrorists' facilities had failed. Although the USA argued that its actions conformed to the rules of necessity and proportionality, there remained considerable international anxiety at the legality of the act and whether just cause existed. Once again the international response to US behaviour was mixed. Pakistan, Russia and most Arab states condemned the act, while the UK and France were more muted in their response.[61]

In all these instances, states justified their action by referring to Article 51. In practice their actions appear more like retaliation than defence. This is a problem since states have generally accepted that retaliation is contrary to international law. This was illustrated by UNSC resolution 188 of 1964, which criticized the UK's reprisals against Yemen as unlawful and contrary to the UN Charter. Past experience suggests, however, that states believe that as long as they invoke Article 51, their actions acquire a veneer of legality. The polarization between states as to what is meant by the right to self-defence threatens to undermine the credibility of the UN and of international law.

While there has always been a tendency by states to interpret the UN Charter creatively, this trend has become more noticeable since the end of the Cold War. In part this is because of the emergence of new security threats which were not envisaged by the Charter. Yet it also reflects the difficulties inherent within the UN system. As one editorial noted in 1993: 'The lesson of the Cold War, finally, was not that the evolution of the UN into a global policeman was thwarted, but that the difficulties and dangers of intervention were masked by the Security Council's paralysis.'[62] The paradox is that states justify their unilateral action by invoking Article 51 of the Charter. The Security Council has sometimes condemned such action, but it has never been able to prevent it. The experience of the League of Nations provides a sombre warning to the UN of the risks that it faces if it is unable to get its authority accepted by its member states.

Implications for the just war tradition

How then should just war ethicists respond to these developments? Are there situations of extreme moral necessity which justify statesmen acting outside or even contrary to the law? If so, what are the implications of widening the interpretation of just cause or other just war criteria such as last resort and right intent?[63]

Many of the current threats to international peace and security have parallels with those faced by rulers in the sixteenth century. Rather than seeking to develop further the just war tradition, scholars and ethicists need only rediscover and adapt what was said in the past. Hugo Grotius' contribution to the just war tradition is of particular relevance. Grotius' *De Jure Belli ac Pacis* contains elements of a medieval doctrine of intervention.[64] In Book II, Grotius examines the quasi-judicial use of war as a police measure against the immoral and the waging of war on behalf of those who are oppressed. Both of these concepts have parallels with current state practice, and need further examination

The idea of taking up arms to punish the wicked characterized the thought and practice of most religions and empires during the sixteenth and seventeenth century. While Grotius argued it was wrong to use force against those who refused to accept Christianity, he accepted the right to use force in an offensive manner to punish evil. Grotius relied on both scriptural and secular authority to argue that the sovereign had a right to punish those sovereign rulers who committed injuries against their subjects or those who 'excessively violate the law of nature or of nations in regard to any persons whatsoever'.[65]

Grotius' position reflected the stance taken by earlier just war ethicists. The law of nature to which Grotius referred informed early Christian belief in the existence of a 'universal moral community of mankind' whose members enjoy reciprocal rights and duties not because of their belonging to a state, but because they belong to a universal community.[66] St Ambrose wrote:

> He who does not keep harm of a friend, if he can, is as much in fault as he who causes it. Wherefore holy Moses gave this as a first proof of his fortitude in war. For when he saw an Hebrew receiving hard treatment at the hands of an Egyptian, he defended him, and laid low the Egyptian and hid him in the sand.[67]

Gentili used this position to adopt a cosmopolitan view of the world. He argued that 'the subjects of others do not seem to me to be outside of that kinship of nature and the society formed by the whole world'. Gentili's view of sovereignty suggested there needed to be some restraints on the sovereign 'unless we wish to make sovereigns exempt from the law and bound by no statutes and no precedents'.[68]

Grotius developed Gentili's thinking in two ways. To Grotius, intervention was a legal right rather than a moral duty and this right could only be exercised once a sovereign had violated the hypothetical rights of his subjects.

> If, however, the wrong is obvious, in case some Busiris, Phalaris, or Thracian Diomede, should inflict upon his subject some treatment as no one is warranted in inflicting, the exercise of the right vested in human society is not precluded . . . If, further, it should be granted that even in extreme need subjects cannot justifiably take up arms . . . nevertheless it will not follow that others may not take up arms on their behalf . . . Hence, Seneca thinks that I may make war upon one who is not one of my own people but oppresses his own, as we said when dealing with the infliction of punishment; a procedure which is often connected with the protection of innocent persons. We know, it is true, from both ancient and modern history, that the desire for what is another's seeks such pretexts as this for its own ends; but a right does not at once cease to exist in case it is to some extent abused by evil men.[69]

In those instances where citizens lack the capacity to redress the situation, a sovereign is entitled to intervene against another sovereign to assert the rights of the oppressed subjects.

This thinking was lost with the Treaty of Westphalia, and the subsequent rise of positivism in international law.

> As positivism displaced scholasticism in international legal theory, and the balance of power came to dominate international relations in Europe, the excision of theology and arguably ethics from international law saw sovereignty emerge as its constituent and increasingly inviolable element.[70]

Positivism led to the rejection of those natural law principles crucial to Grotius' jurisprudence. It also divorced international law from those principles, which had previously constituted the ethics of the individual. This trend was cemented by the virtual fetishization of the state as a morally free entity, in which the sovereign was immune from accountability. The UN Charter reflects this tradition by subordinating human rights and dignity to state sovereignty.

The current inconsistency between international law and state practice has parallels with certain areas of domestic law, most notably the way many legal systems deal with euthanasia. Ian Brownlie, an international legal expert, writes:

> In such a case the possibility of abuse is recognised by the legal policy (that the activity is classified as unlawful) but . . . in very clear cases the law allows mitigation. The father who smothers his severely abnormal child after several years of devoted attention may not be sent to prison, but he is not immune from prosecution and punishment. The euthanasia parallel is useful since it indicates that moderation is allowed for in social systems even when the principle remains firm. Moderation in application does not display a legislative intent to cancel the principle so applied.[71]

While there might be certain uses of force like humanitarian intervention or anticipatory self-defence which remain outside the law, the decision by the UN to offer nominal sanction of such actions recognizes the moral necessity but not the legality of such interventions.

If this analogy is accepted, then it raises the question as to when it is ethical and desirable to intervene in the internal affairs of another nation state. For, as Tony Blair acknowledged at the time of the Kosovo crisis, 'The most pressing foreign policy problem we face is to identify the circumstances in which we should get actively involved in other people's conflicts.' In a major foreign policy speech during the Kosovo crisis, Tony Blair stated:

> If we wanted to right every wrong that we see in the modern world then we would do little else than intervene in the affairs of other countries. We would not be able to cope. So how do we decide when and whether to intervene? I think we need to bear in mind five major considerations.
>
> First, are we sure of our case? War is an imperfect instrument for righting humanitarian distress; but armed force is sometimes the only means of dealing with dictators. Second, have we exhausted all diplomatic options? We should always give peace every chance, as we have in the case of Kosovo. Third, on the basis of a practical assessment of the situation, are there military operations we can sensibly and prudently undertake? Fourth, are we prepared for the long term? In the past we talked too much of exit strategies. But having made a commitment we cannot simply walk away once the fight is over; better to stay with moderate numbers of troops than return for repeat performances with large numbers. And finally, do we have national interest involved? The mass expulsion of ethnic Albanians from Kosovo demanded the notice of the rest of the world. But it does make a difference that this is taking place in such a combustible part of Europe.
>
> I am not suggesting that these are absolute tests. But they are the kind of issues we need to think about in deciding in the future when and whether we will intervene.[72]

Blair's criteria and conditions have obvious parallels with the just war tradition. The first echoes the language of just cause while the second implies that intervention should only be an instrument of last resort, and the third suggests that interventions should only be undertaken if there is a reasonable chance of success. The fifth test could be read as implying that the end of any military intervention must be peace. Blair's final test raises the question of a state's intention.

The Foreign Secretary refined Blair's Doctrine of the International Community in July 2000.[73] He started from the premise that any intervention is an acknowledgement that prevention had failed. States therefore had to invest more in the culture of conflict prevention. While the primary responsibility for preventing violence rests with the state in which it occurs, he recognized that in those instances where a state was incapable of doing so or where the state was complicit in actively promoting the violence then the international community had a responsibility to intervene. Drawing on the lessons of Kosovo, the Foreign Secretary stipulated that since no state should reserve for itself the right to act on behalf of the international community, it was desirable that any use of force should be collective. While these developments do not escape the problem that interfering in the internal affairs of another nation remains contrary to the Charter, they do provide a useful framework through which to evaluate whether the use of force is both ethical and desirable.

Blair's framework may provide a useful starting point for establishing a similar framework of moral reasoning to assist the international community in determining when it is ethical and desirable to resort to anticipatory self-defence or pre-emptive military action. Such a development appears desirable given the suspicion and mistrust surrounding the publication of the US Security Strategy document of September 2002 and its application against Iraq in 2003.[74] There is an obvious need to grapple with the problem of whether it is possible to claim – and so legitimate pre-emptive military action – 'that in the hands of certain states, the mere possession of weapons of mass destruction constitutes an aggression – or, at the very least, an aggression waiting to happen'.[75]

A number of US theologians and ethicists like Richard Regan, James Turner Johnston, Michael Novak and George Weigel have sought to show how the just war tradition can be refined to take account of the threat posed by rogue regimes, terrorists and weapons of mass destruction. Their starting point is the recognition that, 'The exigencies of the current situation require us to think outside the Westphalian box, but to do so in such a way as to avoid dismantling *de facto* the distinction between *bellum* and *duellum*.'[76] By thinking outside the box and escaping the ethical limitations of positivism in international law it is possible to show how traditional just war theory can be used to address the security challenges of the twenty-first century. By escaping the limitations of a Westphalian mindset, it is possible to reclaim classical just war reasoning.

Regan argues that since the just war tradition has always allowed anticipatory self-defence (i.e. defence against an imminent attack) then a state 'need not wait until a would be aggressor nation has stockpiled nuclear or chemical weapons before the potential victim has just cause to strike plants producing such weapons of mass destruction'.[77] Regan, like Weigel, applies this same principle to those states which support terrorist organizations: 'Victim nations need not wait until foreign based or foreign supported terrorists actually attack nationals before they have just cause to use military force against nations harbouring or supporting terrorist organisations and activities.'[78]

To Weigel the crucial issue is not so much weapons of mass destruction or terrorism, as it is the regime factor, 'for weapons of mass destruction are clearly not instances of aggression waiting to happen when they are possessed by stable, law abiding states'.[79] If a regime-centred analysis is accepted,

> then pre-emptive military action to deny the rogue state that kind of destructive capacity would not contravene the defence against aggression concept of just cause. Indeed, it would do precisely the opposite, by giving the concept of defence against aggression real traction in the world we must live in, and transform.[80]

While some argue that anticipatory self-defence is contrary to the UN Charter, Weigel suggests that 'the Charter does not claim for the Security Council sole authority to legitimate the use of armed force'.[81] To do so would be to give the Security Council a moral and political veto over a state's right to self-defence. Weigel therefore sees anticipatory self-defence and pre-emptive military action as a natural and logical extension of Article 51. While it might be politically and militarily desirable for states to build coalitions when using force there is no moral imperative from a just war perspective. But, as Weigel acknowledges, 'Defining the boundaries of unilateral action while defending its legitimacy under certain circumstances is one crucial task for developing just war tradition.'[82]

The recognized danger of using anticipatory self-defence to legitimate military action is that it raises questions as to whether the use of military force pre-empts other methods of conflict resolution. It is plain that unless there is clear and compelling evidence that a state's behaviour threatens another state, then military force should be eschewed. As Regan argues, since anticipatory self-defence or pre-emptive action is itself a breach of the peace, states must have a high degree of moral and practical certitude about the hostile intentions of a potential aggressor.[83] Although mathematical calculations never sit easily with the just war theory, Regan suggests a better than 90 per cent probability. In contrast, Weigel suggests a more normative approach:

> As for rogue states developing or deploying weapons of mass destruction, a developed just war tradition would recognise that here, too, last resort cannot be understood mathematically, as the terminal point in a lengthy series of non-military alternatives. Can we not say that last resort has been satisfied when a rogue state has made plain, by its conduct, that it holds international law in contempt, and when it can be demonstrated that the threat it poses is likely, and when it can be demonstrated that the threat the rogue state poses is intensifying?[84]

This raises the circular question as to who or what ought to determine whether or not a state's behaviour warrants the title rogue regime. This once again comes back to the issue of proper authority. While Weigel and others would argue that the lack of a fully formed international political community vests such responsibility in the state, others would argue that such autonomy risks a global descent into chaos.

There are clear criteria regulating humanitarian intervention, but the ethics of anticipatory self-defence remain fluid. This fluidity, reflective of the contestability of moral, political and legal boundaries, suggests the need for further ethical reflection. Many would argue that these ethical debates highlight all that is morally dubious about the just war tradition, in that the tradition appears to be so elastic in its interpretation as to justify any state action. Does it matter that those ethicists advocating a further development in just war thinking are based in the USA?

It is equally clear from the preceding analysis that the just war tradition is a dynamic rather than a static theory, which has developed over time as a result of sustained dialogue as to the ethics of war. Faced with new security threats, it is hardly surprising that the just war tradition is being further developed. What is perhaps surprising, as will be shown in subsequent chapters, is that European theologians have appeared to be reluctant to enter the debate.

Conclusion

The overriding concern of the just war theory is to ensure the primacy of peace over war. War has no intrinsic moral value in and of itself. The legitimacy of making and waging war is entirely dependent on its ability to restore peaceful relations between states. In this sense both the *jus ad bellum* and *jus in bello* branches of just war theory are subordinate to a wider *jus in pace*. If the aim of war is peace then it is incumbent on those who wage war to articulate the peace for which war is being fought. The peace to which just war theory alludes is neither some purely military victory nor the mere absence of violence, but the restoration of community. Justified warfare is warfare which recognizes that the unity of humanity has been broken either by an act of aggression or oppression, and that non-coercive attempts to remedy the brokenness of human relations has been found wanting and that alternative methods are both necessary and desirable.

A just war is one that leads to the realization of community. As Coates records, the type of community for which war is being fought is all-important. An imperial order where one state seeks to dominate another is not a just and well-ordered community, because it requires the victory of one community over another. From a Christian perspective community alludes to the unity of humanity, where the 'world as a whole . . . is in a way a single state'.[85] While this community may still not be fully realized, this vision of community stands as testament to the hope of an ecumenical rather than an imperial order. A peace that promotes the particularistic agenda of a single nation state over and above a peace which furthers the international common good is contrary to both the spirit and the letter of the just war tradition.

Just war theory, it could be argued, seeks to bridge the gap between the Old and New Testament, between political idealism and political realism. It is neither 'realist' nor 'pacifist', but rather shares elements of both. While idealists see the theory as no more than the legitimization of war, realists see it as placing unnecessary ethical and moral restraints on a nation's ability to wage war, which could undermine the national interest. Yet the territory of the just war tradition lies precisely between these two competing perspectives. It sets out the grounds on which war is permitted and the limits beyond which it would be unjustified. It binds both the idealist and the realist together in a dialectical relationship, by providing a common language and agreed reference points, so sustaining a continuing critical dialogue between competing traditions.

Just war thinking is not about rationalizing war, but about setting the limits within which war must confine itself and outside which it must cease, whatever the consequences. Thus, it is perfectly possible for a just war to be fought unjustly and for an unjust war to be fought in strict accordance with the rules of war. Similarly, it does not offer absolutes, suggesting instead that any use of military force must be continually re-evaluated against declared aims and means. As most military studies acknowledge, aims and means can change over time. The fluidity and dualism of *jus ad bellum* and *jus in bello* is at the very heart of all that is most problematic in the moral reality of war. In some instances the selective use of just war thinking and the failure of some political commentators to properly distinguish between *jus ad bellum* and *jus in bello* can undermine its utility as a framework of analysis.

Some have argued that the tradition has become outdated because the problems facing nation states no longer follow traditional models of warfare, as involving two or more nations. Others have argued that it needs to be updated to take account of the spate of intra-state conflicts which have marred international relations since the end of the Cold War. Such debates are not new. Just war theorists have for centuries been forced to re-examine the tradition's basic tenets in the light of major developments such as the emergence of the nation state as well as the advent of modern methods of warfare. In other words it is a dynamic rather than a static way of thinking. Whatever its fate, the future of just war thinking is dependent on the resonance of arguments employed both for and against it.

Many of the current threats to international peace and security, and the ethical dilemmas they raise, have parallels with classical just war tradition. The creation of the state system and the drift towards positivism in international law saw a separation of ethics from law. It is evident from state practice that since the end of the Cold War there has seen a counter trend where ethics once again plays a crucial role in determining the political use of force. Escaping the limitations of positivism ought to be welcomed. The trend towards humanitarian intervention and anticipatory self-defence mirror Grotius' recommendation that force should be used to punish evil and relieve oppression. Seen from this perspective the current use of force more clearly resembles quasi-police action than it does traditional nineteenth- or twentieth-century models of warfare.

The just war tradition is by necessity morally ambiguous and tends to see conflict as inescapable and part of the human condition. It should not therefore be seen as a set of law-like propositions within a frame of empirical theory. Just war theory holds to a moral reality of war and suggests that there are values, such as the defence of the innocent, which can and ought to be protected by the use of force. As a result it is more than just a theory about war, it is a theory of international and domestic politics, which sets the political within a context of moral concerns and considerations. As will be illustrated in subsequent chapters the way in which the just war tradition is used by a range of actors reveals much about their overall world-views.

The inescapability of interpretation, the contestability of political and moral concepts, as well as the fixity and fluidity of language means that the boundaries between morality and politics, between religious and non-religious actors become increasingly blurred when issues of war and peace are debated. As the following chapters on the First and Second Gulf Wars illustrate, more often than not politicians will find themselves debating with religious leaders, both drawing on the same just war terminology in which to argue their case about the legitimacy or morality of a particular use of force. The ensuing moral political discourse generated by such interactions is encouraging since it provides a warning against attempts to dissociate the practice of government from ethics.

The following chapters examine the use of the just war tradition at the time of the First and Second Gulf Wars. It particularly focuses on how British churches approached the issue of war and peace. What does their use of the just war theory reveal as to their world-views and their understanding of international relations in a post-Cold War age? How have the churches reacted to the emergence of new security threats? To what extent have churches, the moral guardians of the just war tradition, helped to shape the wider political debate as to when it is ethical to use force in the pursuit of justice?

4 | Triumph without Victory: The First Gulf War, 1990–1991

> What is at stake is more than one small country; it is a big idea: a new world order – where diverse nations are drawn together in common cause, to achieve the universal aspirations of mankind – peace and security, freedom and the rule of law.[1]

Iraq's invasion of Kuwait on 2 August 1990 was a defining moment in global politics. The nature of the international community's response would show how far the hopes raised by the ending of the Cold War had been realized. The question was not so much whether Iraq's aggression would be challenged, but rather the means (sanctions, diplomacy or force) by which Iraqi forces would be removed from Kuwait. This chapter examines the ethical and political debates which preceded Operation Desert Storm. The decision to use force and the way the war was conducted were seen to offer a model for the new world order, setting the standards for the use of force by the great powers in a post-Cold War era. Such force as was used against Iraq was sanctioned by the United Nations and conducted by an international coalition in pursuit of limited objectives. The military option was pursued only after other means had failed. The use of precision-guided weaponry and the care taken to avoid civilian casualties suggest the coalition did not lose sight of the distinction between combatants and non-combatants.

The debates that marked the First Gulf War were characterized by just war language. On the eve of war Prime Minister John Major said:

> Let us never forget that the decision to use force was first taken by Saddam Hussein . . . when he chose to invade Kuwait. We do not want a conflict. We are not thirsting for war, but if it comes I believe that it would be a just war. However great the costs of such a war might be, they would be less than those that we would face if we failed to stand up for the principle of what is right, and to stand up for it now.[2]

The British churches did not all agree with this analysis. Although the Scottish and Irish churches unequivocally condemned the war, English churches found it harder to come to a conclusion as to the war's morality. The Church of England's House of Bishops hesitated right up to the eve of war itself, before it reluctantly accepted that the war might indeed be just. These deliberations led some to accuse the Church of 'culpable failure' by 'failing to give a spiritual and moral lead' to the nation.[3] Others questioned whether this corporate silence suggested the Church had nothing useful to say about the war.[4]

This chapter examines the British domestic debate at the time of the First Gulf War. Why was there such a lack of agreement within and between churches, as well as between churches and the Government, as to the morality of war against Iraq? While it is not suggested that churches should necessarily say the same thing, it is important to examine whether the diversity of views represented a difference of perceptions and understandings in the use of the just war tradition. Similarly, while it is not uncommon for churches to disagree with governments it is important to examine whether the use of just war language by politicians simply reflected an appropriation of religious language for narrowly conceived political objectives, which the churches rightly opposed? Or did the problem lie with the churches' own understanding and interpretation of what constituted a just war? Why did some churches find it relatively easy to reach a judgement on the war, while others continued to keep their options open until the last moment?

The end of the Cold War

It is difficult to explain the international community's response to Iraq's invasion of Kuwait without understanding the wider international environment. The Gulf crisis represented a microcosm of issues at the heart of international affairs. Despite the simmering crisis in the Gulf, world opinion was focused on European developments. Politicians were still trying to assess the full implications of the Velvet Revolutions of 1989, in which the popular outpourings of decades of pent-up frustration resulted in the crumbling of communism across Eastern Europe symbolized by the collapse of the Berlin Wall. The dominant issues of the old order, such as the strategic rivalry between East and West, gave way to a new security agenda marked by the revival of ethnic and national tensions within the Balkan and Caucasian Republics. The threat of total war that had dominated Europe for nearly half a century had abated. In its place emerged the threat of low-intensity conflicts in Africa and Eastern Europe.

The optimism surrounding the events of 1989–90 led Western governments to believe that the end of the superpower rivalry would make future conflicts easier to handle. Initial efforts to restructure the regional and international security apparatus saw agreement on German reunification, the revival of the Western European Union as the defence arm of the European Community, and the strengthening of pan-European institutions, such as the Conference on Security and Cooperation in Europe (CSCE). Discussions were also underway to create a European Political Union following the signing of the Maastricht Treaty in 1992.

Efforts to improve European co-operation were accompanied by a reawakening of historical anxieties. Margaret Thatcher remained apprehensive that the USA would eschew its 'special relationship' with the UK in favour of a reunified Germany. Similarly, France feared Germany would usurp its leadership role within Europe. There was also the realization that the United States had emerged as the dominant power – economically, politically and militarily. The unspoken question was whether the USA would retreat into isolation or whether it would continue to be engaged in world affairs.

These discussions between European states were reflected in developments by European church organizations. As early as 1990 the Conference of European Churches and the Ecumenical Commission for Church and Society in the European Communities were examining the potential of a merger.[5] In Britain efforts to develop a more inclusive ecumenical structure led to the replacement, in 1990, of the British Council of Churches with the Council of Churches for Britain and Ireland, of which the Roman Catholic Church in England, Scotland and Wales was a full member. There was optimism that historical divisions and animosities could be replaced by a new spirit of ecumenical co-operation and unity. The end of the Cold War contributed to a more optimistic atmosphere and the perceived role of churches and other parts of civil society in developing a widespread feeling that situations of major social and political conflict, such as apartheid in South Africa, could be resolved peacefully.[6]

In the Middle East, the end of the Cold War deprived the Arab world of one of its traditional allies, the USSR. In Iraq, the end of superpower patronage led to a growing realization, by President Saddam Hussein, that Iraq's deep economic crisis following the Iran–Iraq war, and its dependence upon overseas credit, could only be resolved by increasing its revenues. The quest for additional national resources in the shape of Kuwaiti oil was the determining factor in Iraq's invasion of Kuwait. If Iraq thought the West would turn a blind eye to such naked aggression, as it had in the past, then it had failed to properly understand the implications of the end of the Cold War. The West could no longer overlook Iraq's human rights abuses and the threat to regional destabilization posed by the enormous share of Iraq's GNP being spent on military industrialization projects.

Responding to aggression

Iraq's invasion of Kuwait violated the most fundamental norms of international law. It represented the only case in the UN's history of an attempted annexation of an entire state that was a recognized member of the international community. It was a flagrant act of aggression that contravened Article 2 of the UN Charter. As Margaret Thatcher stated: 'Iraq's invasion of Kuwait defies every principle for which the United Nations stands. If we let it succeed, no small country can ever feel safe again. The law of the jungle would take over from the rule of law.'[7]

Within a few days the international community moved beyond issuing condemnatory statements to imposing full and comprehensive sanctions against Iraq. This was a natural response to Iraq's muted reply to UNSC resolution 660. Iraq's dependence upon a single commodity – oil, which accounted for some 95 per cent of its exports – made it particularly susceptible to economic pressure.[8] Sanctions were enforced by UNSCR 665 authorizing the setting up of a naval blockade to prohibit the movement of goods into and out of Iraq.[9] By 6 August King Fahd of Saudi Arabia had agreed to the deployment of a multinational force on Saudi territory. This action was a defensive measure to counter and deter the menacing Iraqi military build-up on the Saudi border.[10]

The international community's quick response to the invasion reflected international anxiety at Iraq's behaviour. Iraq's repression within Kuwait revealed the regime's debased nature and Saddam Hussein's willingness to flout international norms and behaviour governing the conduct of war.[11] This repression contributed to refugee flows to neighbouring countries, which threatened to destabilize the wider Middle East. At the same time Western public opinion became inflamed by the perceived ill-treatment of fellow nationals held hostage by Iraq, which also sought to use foreign nationals as a form of protection against any immediate retaliation.[12]

From a just war perspective Iraq's invasion and subsequent rape of Kuwait, combined with the human rights atrocities contributing to a refugee crisis, constituted an evil which needed to be resisted and reversed. Whatever the legitimacy of Iraq's grievances against Kuwait, it seemed less interested in absorbing Kuwait than in dismantling it, thereby threatening its viability as an independent sovereign nation. This, combined with Iraq's threatening behaviour towards Saudi Arabia, meant that Iraq's aggression could not be left unchecked.

The deployment of a multinational force to Saudi Arabia was purely a defensive measure. The decision to use economic coercion to reinforce diplomatic statements was both a necessary and proportionate measure aimed at resolving the crisis peacefully. The changed international environment following the end of the Cold War made an international response via the UN both necessary and possible. The UN's involvement indicated that the international community's efforts resembled a form of quasi police action, in that it sought to uphold international law and agreed standards of behaviour.

The UK played a constructive role in the early days of the crisis. Margaret Thatcher was in the USA at the time of the invasion of Kuwait. She advised the President to take a firm stand. Thatcher's close relationship with Bush, and the emphasis she placed on the UK's special relationship with the USA meant that from the start UK policy closely mirrored that of the USA. The Foreign Secretary, Douglas Hurd, announced, on 8 August, the Government's decision to 'contribute forces to a multinational effort for the collective defence of the territory of Saudi Arabia and other threatened states in the area, and in support of the United Nations embargo'.[13] On 11 September 1990 the Cabinet Overseas and Defence Committee agreed to the deployment of the Seventh Armoured Brigade.

The Government's nervousness about public opinion in the face of this military commitment led to the recall of Parliament on 6 September. Before the recall, political debate had been conducted largely through the media. The churches contributed to this debate by releasing initial statements.[14] These statements recognized that Iraq's invasion of Kuwait violated international law and needed to be resisted, but that such resistance needed to be co-ordinated through the United Nations. There was a shared concern that Iraq's behaviour would elicit an ill-considered reaction from the West which might lead to an escalation of the crisis. For this reason there was wide ecumenical support for the action taken by the UN Security Council in imposing sanctions on Iraq. In the first month of the crisis the churches therefore emphasized a dual policy of containment and conflict management by the UN. Apart from responding to the immediacy of the political crisis, the churches contributed to the humanitarian relief exercise in Jordan and surrounding Gulf countries by supporting emergency appeals issued by Christian Aid, CAFOD and Tearfund.

Parliament's recall allowed the bishops in the Upper House to engage in a fuller consideration of the crisis than was possible in a press release. During the House of Lords' debate, the Archbishop of Canterbury, the Most Revd Robert Runcie, argued that Iraq's invasion of Kuwait amounted to 'naked aggression' that needed to be 'vigorously resisted'. Iraq's treatment of Western hostages was seen as a 'flagrant violation of international law'. However, he urged caution and the need to avoid taking any measures which might further inflame the situation. The fate of Western hostages should not be the decisive factor in determining government policy. International resistance needed to stop short of military action, until 'we give sanctions time to work', or until such time as the 'Iraqis took further aggressive steps'.[15]

This message was consistent with government policy as well as the position previously agreed by churches. Dr Runcie agreed with the Prime Minister, Margaret Thatcher, that sanctions must be given 'a few months' to work. However, he was less equivocal than the Government on the steps that might be necessary if, after a 'few months', sanctions had proved ineffective. The Defence Secretary, Tom King, was clear: 'While we seek the implementation of the UN resolutions by peaceful means, other options remain available and, one way or another, he will lose.'[16]

The logic of offensive action

The most contentious issue surrounding Operation Desert Storm was not the question of just cause, but rather last resort. These debates became more heated when, following the Congressional elections on 6 November, President Bush doubled the number of US troops in the Gulf. Bush's decision seemed contrary to the Administration's earlier optimism.

> Now we are starting to see evidence that the sanctions are pinching. So what should we say, 'Okay, gave 'em two months, didn't work. Let's get on with it and kill a whole bunch of people?' That's crazy. That's crazy . . .[17]

The decision to abandon economic and diplomatic means to resolve the crisis led many to accuse the USA and the UK of acting prematurely. This invariably led to a questioning of the motives driving US policy.

The decision to prepare for the offensive option arose from the interplay of a number of domestic and international factors. Fundamental to both London and Washington was the need to reverse Iraq's aggression:

> Sanctions will take time to have their full-intended effect. We shall continue to review all options with our allies, but let it be clear, we will not let this aggression stand. Iraq will not be permitted to annex Kuwait. And that's not a threat, it's not a boast, it's just the way it's going to be.[18]

The twin planks in Bush's concept of a 'New World Order' were the principles of non-aggression and non-appeasement. It was felt that even if Iraq could be persuaded to vacate Kuwait, Iraq would still pose a threat to regional and international security. As Dick Cheney, the US Secretary of State for Defence, said:

> My own personal view is that it is far better to deal with Saddam Hussein, while the coalition is intact, while we have the United Nations behind us . . . than it will be to deal with him in five to ten years from now . . . when Saddam Hussein has become an even better armed and more threatening regional superpower than he is at present.[19]

A factor therefore in the calculations leading to Operation Desert Storm was the understanding that Iraq's 'capacity for future aggression must be part of any settlement with Iraq'.[20] While sanctions over a longer term might have reversed Iraqi aggression, only military force would reduce Iraq's military capacity so preventing future expansionism. Iraq's voluntary withdrawal from Kuwait was increasingly seen as the 'nightmare scenario'.

In moving to an offensive strategy, the Bush administration took a pessimistic view as to the utility of sanctions. Although sanctions played a significant role in isolating Iraq, it became evident that sanctions would not prove a quick solution.[21] The US State Department statistics indicated that while sanctions would result in a sharp decline in industrial productivity, Iraq's ability to stockpile spare parts would enable it to buy time.[22] Washington's concern, shared by other members of the coalition, most noticeably the UK, was that the longer Iraq stayed in Kuwait the harder it would become to maintain Arab support for the coalition. The confrontation between Israeli soldiers and Palestinian protestors on 8 October 1990 outside the Al-Aqsa Mosque, in which 21 Palestinians were killed and more than 100 wounded highlighted the potential divisions within the coalition.[23] With Saddam Hussein playing the Arab card by accusing the West of double standards, there was always the danger that such linkage would restrict the use of options other than sanctions.[24]

Even in the short term, Iraq's response to economic and diplomatic coercion hardly inspired confidence. Iraq's rejection of successive UN resolutions indicated that prolonging the time devoted to the diplomatic and economic route would reward Iraq for its illegal behaviour. The longer Iraq remained in Kuwait the harder it would become to restore the al-Sabhad family. Reports suggest that Bush was deeply affected by accounts of looting and torture within Kuwait and concluded that Iraq aimed to destroy the state of Kuwait.[25] Furthermore, by late October 1990 Saddam Hussein had called for a jihad against the Saudi royal family and the Mubarak Government in Cairo. There was clear Arab consternation that failure to resolve these issues quickly could result in long-term regional instability.

Given these considerations the US and UK strategy was one of no negotiation. As John Major indicated, the international community would not accept the partial withdrawal or 'artificial linkage to solutions of other problems'.[26] It would insist, rather, on an 'absolute commitment to implement the Security Council's resolutions in full and without delay'.[27] This policy aimed to maintain the pressure on Saddam Hussein while also allowing him the choice of pursuing any of the options being offered by the UN or various Arab delegations.

This is not to suggest that diplomatic initiatives to avert war were absent. On 30 November, the day after securing UNSC resolution 678, providing all necessary authority to reverse Iraq's aggression, Bush announced his willingness to go the 'extra mile for peace' by holding talks with the Iraqi Government.[28] There was little optimism that such talks would break the impasse, but the move was important in showing 'to the American people and to others . . . that we left no stone unturned in the search for peace'.[29] Unfortunately, the talks between Secretary of State James Baker and the Iraqi Deputy Prime Minister Tariq Aziz in Geneva on 9 January 1991 merely highlighted the diplomatic gulf between Iraq and the international community.

Rather than using the Geneva talks to offer a partial withdrawal, which would have split the allied coalition and undermined popular support in the USA and the UK for military action, Iraq held to its original position that Kuwait was the nineteenth province of Iraq. This bluster characterized Iraq's diplomatic blunders throughout the crisis. Rather than meeting with President Mubarak and President Assad in January 1991, Saddam Hussein sought to undermine Middle Eastern peace initiatives by appropriating pan-Arab and pan-Islamic symbols while simultaneously calling for the overthrow of various Arab rulers.

Iraq's failure to comply with the UN's deadline of 16 January 1991 left the allied coalition with little option but to use force. A prudential decision was taken that only a properly authorized use of force would secure the UN's objectives. The decision not to persist with sanctions or to continue with negotiations did not violate the just war tradition of last resort. Iraq's pillaging of Kuwait and the threats issued against other Middle Eastern states suggested that to persist with non-violent methods of conflict resolution might prove counter-productive. To delay military action ran the risk of jeopardizing the coalition's unity and with it the chance of securing the just end for which war was finally fought.

Just war theory requires that all reasonable efforts are made before recourse to military action. The unprecedented international economic and political activity that followed Iraq's invasion of

Kuwait suggests that this criterion was met. The subjective judgement that further efforts at peacefully resolving the crisis would prove futile did not undermine the efficacy of the decision to use force. This decision was compatible with the spirit of Article 42 of the UN's Charter, which recognizes that the use of armed force is legitimate when the Security Council considers that alternative measures 'would be inadequate or have proved to be inadequate . . . to maintain international peace and security'.

Last resort and proportionality

In responding to the decision to set a deadline for Iraq's withdrawal from Kuwait, the churches did not speak with one voice. While the Church of England and the Roman Catholic Church of England and Wales came to accept, albeit reluctantly, the move to deadline diplomacy, others, like the Church of Scotland, held that military action was premature. The intense debate within the British churches was indicative of a wider theological dispute as to the efficacy of using force as a tool of statecraft.

A five-page press release issued by the Council of Churches for Britain and Ireland (CCBI), following an ecumenical meeting with the Foreign Secretary on 9 January, sets out the churches' reasons for favouring a continuation of the sanctions policy rather than a move to military action:

> The delegation is deeply concerned that the implementation of sanctions, which initially received unprecedented international support, including that of the British and Irish Churches, appears to have been completely taken over by the military option and that military considerations have evidently taken precedence over all other possibilities, including diplomatic efforts . . . Sanctions are not a soft option. They are intended to pressurise by coercion and there is evidence that they have been starting to take effect.[30]

On the question of the possible consequences of war the statement noted:

> the appalling scale of death and destruction in the Middle East region, the effects on the world economy (with the most brutal

results for the poorest nations of the world who are already suffering severely as a result of the crisis), the potentiality of eco-
logical disaster and the new crisis into which political relations
within the region and between the Western world and the
Middle East are all too likely to be placed – have not sufficiently been taken into account in any argument for a military
solution.[31]

The CCBI favoured continuing with a policy of containment, which
it believed would isolate the aggressor while providing space for
dialogue.[32]

The CCBI's position appears to have reflected a quite widespread
opinion within the churches. A survey conducted by ICM on behalf
of the *Sunday Correspondent* showed that 75 per cent of Anglican
clergy and bishops were against the use of military action until sanctions had been given an additional six months to work. More than a
third thought the allies should never start a war. Only 18 per cent
were prepared to say how much loss of life would be justified by the
cause: 4 per cent said less than 100, 5 per cent less than that, but
6 per cent said more than 100,000. However, 35 per cent said that
no loss of life could be justified.[33]

The perceived destructiveness of modern warfare led some
churches and religious leaders to a narrow interpretation of the
criterion of last resort. A letter to *The Times* signed by the Bishop of
Bath and Wells, the Rt Revd George Carey, and 14 other bishops
urged Bush to 'go the extra mile for peace' so as to avoid a 'fearful
loss of life . . . making a graveyard of the Middle East'. It urged
Christians not to remain silent on the issue but instead to join 'a
great movement of prayer' so 'helping to avoid this potentially
terrible conflict'.

The Scottish Episcopal Church made similar predictions: 'The cost
of war in human life and material damage would be far greater than
anything that has already been inflicted by Iraq.'[34] It predicted
1 million civilian casualties and 314,000 military casualties. It believed
that war should be eschewed in favour of other 'crisis management'
techniques, such as 'economic and moral pressure' and 'patient
negotiation'.[35] Similarly, the leader of the Scottish Roman Catholic
Church, Archbishop Winning, echoed the thoughts of his predecessor,
Cardinal Gray, in arguing that the destructiveness of modern warfare
meant that there could be no just war in the present age.

As has been noted, the *jus ad bellum* criterion of proportionality and reasonable chance of success require subjective reasoning based on hypothetical projections as to a war's likely course. It requires a judgement to be made as to whether the cause justifies the loss of life associated with war. So, on what did the churches base their calculations? The Church of Scotland indicated that its predictions were based on consultations with 'a wide spectrum of experts, doctors, lawyers and academics in the field of politics, economics and ecology'. Who were these experts?

An examination of the statement issued by the Church of Scotland shows that Keith Bovey, the Chairman of the Scottish Campaign for Nuclear Disarmament, was among those who advised the Moderator of the General Assembly, the Primus of the Scottish Episcopal Church and the Roman Catholic Archbishop of Glasgow.[36] Other expert opinion was offered by Pax Christi, the Campaign for Nuclear Disarmament, Christian CND, the Medical Campaign Against Nuclear Weapons, the Anglican Pacifist Fellowship, Campaign Against Arms Trade, and the National Peace Council.[37]

These organizations provided the backbone of the churches' peace movement during the Cold War. It is not surprising that they played an important role in shaping Christian attitudes to the First Gulf War. Theologically their position reflected the belief that the use of force was contrary to Jesus' teachings. The decision to deploy US cruise missiles in Western Europe in the early 1980s was highly controversial and led to a huge growth in the 'peace movement' and resurgence in the Campaign for Nuclear Disarmament. Many of those attracted to the peace camp during the Cold War were not biblical pacifists but nuclear and functional pacifists fearful that the possession of nuclear, chemical and biological weapons threatened a holocaust.

The relationship between churches and Christian peace organizations explains much of the alarmist and apocalyptic language used in many church statements. David Bleakley, the President of the Church of England's Church Mission Society, speaking at a TUC rally in Belfast stated:

There are no acceptable grounds for risking a holocaust in the Gulf. Such a military lunge into the unknown would be politically suicidal and devastatingly open ended. We ignore the fact that conventionally controlled warfare has been replaced by technical combinations increasingly beyond human control. With ABC warfare (atomic, biological, chemical) there is no longer an 'All-Clear' which turns off the strife. Indeed, there is no way in which a Gulf War could be confined to Kuwait – it would spread throughout the region killing and maiming millions and sending destabilising shock waves to every nation on earth. Unfortunately, debate on these human issues has been muted in the West and whole nations are being brainwashed into war.[38]

Bleakley's moral and political view stands in some contrast to the essentially speculative and subjective nature of the just war tradition's criterion of proportionality. As one journalist, Paul Barker, noted at the time:

> The essential thing about a war is that nobody can predict or prescribe how it will go, how it will be fought, or how long it will last. Pay no attention to anyone who forecasts how war in the Gulf might work out. The one certain thing is this: they do not know what they are talking about.[39]

Not all British churches adopted a narrow reading of proportionality. Dr Runcie refused to speculate as to the potential number of war casualties. In a speech to the General Synod in November 1990 he said:

> The doctrine of just war has been much invoked and variously interpreted. Sometimes the distortion of the doctrine has gone to extraordinary lengths. For example, some have argued that an essential part of the doctrine is the rule that in a 'just war' non-combatants must not be hurt. That quite frankly is an absurdity, it is a doctrine of near perfection that has been unattainable save in the most exceptional circumstances.[40]

He recognized that despite the advances in military technology and talk of surgical strikes 'if it comes to war in the Gulf, non-combatants will most certainly be killed and maimed and bereaved'. He accepted the danger that Iraq would 'probably use chemical and biological weapons, as it did in the Iran–Iraq war and against their own Kurdish citizens', with the result that combatants and non-combatants would probably suffer 'unspeakable horrors'.[41]

Despite sharing many of the concerns of the churches' peace movement Dr Runcie concluded: 'Despite all the horrors and misery that war would certainly involve, we have to face the fact that it could be the lesser of two evils.'[42] Central to Runcie's thinking was the understanding that Iraq's 'act of naked aggression' needed to be challenged and reversed – peacefully if possible but by force if necessary. In doing so he never lost sight of the fact that 'though war is only rarely just, it can be justifiable':

> Christians have a built-in resistance to the use of force. We are given only one mandate. We are to be peacemakers. But the Bible insists that we live in a world in rebellion against its own best interests, a world which has rejected the order given to it by its creator. Christianity does not lack realism about the intransigence of conflict. The Scriptures speak of our responsibility for seeking justice and the well-being of creation in the world as its exists. The hard fact is that the use of force is caused as much by human virtues – our sense of justice; our belief in the difference between right and wrong; our readiness for self-sacrifice on behalf of others – as it is by any of our failures.[43]

Unlike those in the no-war camp whose understanding of last resort was tied to issues of proportionality and right intent, Dr Runcie offered an alternative, and in many ways a more traditional interpretation of the just war theory, by linking the criterion of last resort to the criterion of just cause. Whereas many within the peace movement saw peace as the mere absence of violence, Dr Runcie saw the pursuit of justice as central to a Christian understanding of peace.

The Archbishop recognized, too, the subjective nature of the *jus ad bellum* criteria of last resort and proportionality. His November General Synod address indicated that such judgements ultimately rest with political, rather than religious, leaders. A number of other Anglican bishops, including the Bishop of Oxford, also favoured this approach.

> In the end, only the governments concerned can decide whether every peaceful means of achieving a resolution has

been tried and failed. Only they can then decide whether a military victory is possible and whether one could be achieved without a disproportionate cost both in terms of human suffering and long term political damage to the whole area.[44]

Rather than seeking to make a judgement as to whether all other options had been found wanting, the Archbishop asked those questions of Government. This shifted the emphasis from the Church of England having to make a judgement on the basis of imperfect and poor information, to the Government having to explain why, if war was considered necessary, other means had failed.[45] By asking these question of Government, the Archbishop adopted an advisory role which worked to the detriment of those in the peace camp who sought an unequivocal position on the Gulf crisis reflective of their own opinion.

Cardinal Hume adopted a similar strategy in seeking to bridge the differences apparent within the Roman Catholic Church in England and Wales. In a letter to *The Times* on 8 November 1990, the Cardinal argued that 'limited military action' against Saddam Hussein could only be morally justified on two conditions. The first was that 'all other avenues to a possible solution' had been tried and failed; and, second, that war should 'not cause physical and political damage out of all proportion to the original injustice'. Rather than listing a range of alternative methods of conflict resolution, the Cardinal made it clear that the responsibility for making such judgements lay with those in political authority, rather than with the churches. Although he recognized the difficulty faced by 'those in authority' in seeking to make such judgements, he was firm in his conclusion that 'failure to observe that duty would certainly render a military intervention immoral'.[46] This position was reflected in a statement by the Catholic Bishops' Conference of England and Wales, read out in all Roman Catholic churches on 2 December 1990, the First Sunday of Advent.[47]

The competing church statements reveal differing uses of the just war tradition. Those churches that linked questions of last resort to those of proportionality downplayed the question of just cause. This was at odds with traditional understandings of the just war tradition. As illustrated in previous chapters, 'the question of proportion must be evaluated . . . from the viewpoint of the hierarchy of strictly moral values', which recognizes that 'there are greater evils than the physical death and destruction wrought in war'.[48] With hindsight Keith Clements, who was then the CCBI's International Affairs Secretary, acknowledged that some churches 'abused the just war tradition' to suit their own political and theological agenda.[49]

The result was to turn the just war theory on its head. Consequently much religious analysis framed the crisis as one of the West initiating war against Iraq. Professor Rowan Williams, then Regius Professor of Theology at Oxford, wrote of a 'war against Iraq started by the US and its allies', while Canon Philip Crowe spoke of the West 'starting a war against Iraq'.[50] Time and energy was therefore spent questioning America's motives in a way which led some people to suspect that their analysis was itself motivated by anti-Americanism. The Bishop of Oxford, for example, said: 'One of the things that worries me at the moment is that there is such an instinctive anti-Americanism in the world. I don't think that one can rule out at least the possibility that this war could be justified.'[51]

Last resort and right intent

The international community's decision to intervene in Kuwait, while refusing to act in other conflicts such as Israel and Palestine, led many to question whether oil was the determining factor in shaping allied policy. The churches' peace wing questioned whether the justness of the cause, evicting Iraq from Kuwait, had been corrupted by national self-interest. An open letter from Philip Crowe and Rowan Williams to the Church of England's House of Bishops provides a good example of this reasoning. Crowe and Williams did not deny that Iraq's invasion of Kuwait was wrong, but the existence of other factors, such as oil, led them to question the real motives of the allies:

> Iraq's invasion of Kuwait is a great evil. No one questions that, apart from Iraq. But it is also a serious tactical error. It has given Western nations the excuse to continue to act out of self-interest, but to do so in the name of international justice.[52]

They went on to challenge the Government's portrayal of the crisis as a battle between 'good' and 'evil'. 'If one's own side is not the embodiment of good, then neither is one's enemy the embodiment of evil.' Both were concerned that by demonizing 'the other' a non-violent resolution of the conflict was rendered practically impossible.

The open letter to the House of Bishops rehearsed a number of arguments characteristic of the wider peace camp.

- Western complicity in creating and manipulating national boundaries in the Middle East had contributed to the Iran–Iraq war as well as Iraq's invasion of Kuwait.
- The silence of the UK and the USA in the face of Iraq's use of chemical weapons during the Iran–Iraq war reflected the West's regional interest in seeing Iran weakened.
- To respond to Iraq's invasion of Kuwait, while leaving unresolved other injustices, such as Israel's occupation of the West Bank, was an example of selective justice and double standards.
- Preparations for war were seen as indicative of the West's dependence on 'the resources we need to maintain an artificially high standard of living. Does anyone seriously believe that the international force would be in the Gulf at all if Kuwait produced carrots and Saudi Arabia was one vast onion bed?'

Where Crowe and Williams departed from the peace camp was in their recognition that there were circumstances in which a war with Iraq might be the lesser of two evils. These included the prolongation of the status quo leading to either an erosion of UN sanctions or further Iraqi aggression. They remained adamant however that Christians should be under no illusion that it would not be a 'simple war in defence of justice and freedom'.[53]

There is no doubt that the factors listed by Crowe and Williams were significant subsidiary factors in government thinking. The Government sought to prevent an unfriendly power like Iraq from controlling decisions on the output and price of the West's oil imports from the Gulf. An Iraqi monopoly of Middle Eastern oil would have disrupted the world economy, threatening European jobs and livelihoods. Moreover, Iraq's invasion of Kuwait created uncertainty in the markets, which threatened to undermine British Middle Eastern exports. Additionally, the Gulf War provided the UK with an opportunity to demonstrate its continued relevance within the transatlantic alliance.

Did these subsidiary concerns undermine the justification for military action against Iraq? They remained secondary rather than primary concerns. The 'blood for oil' argument de-emphasized Iraq's aggression against Kuwait and restoration of the legitimate Kuwaiti Government. The 'blood for oil' argument also ignored the need to preserve the wider international peace and security in the region by disarming Iraq of its weapons of mass destruction. Oil was the determining factor in the crisis, but only in so far as it provided the catalyst for Iraq's invasion of Kuwait.

Contrary to some reports claiming that the Gulf War reflected US imperial ambitions, the overriding consideration in the build-up to Operation Desert Storm was the attempt to uphold the principle of non-aggression.[54] The limited objective of the allied coalition – the expulsion of Iraq from Kuwait – excluded the possibility of over-throwing Saddam Hussein. This was necessary in order to assuage the concerns of the Soviet Union and China as well as other Arab states. Douglas Hurd told the House of Commons on 15 January 1991: 'there is no hidden agenda. There is no intention to dismember Iraq. There is no intention to impose on Iraq a Government or President of our choice.'[55]

The legal basis for war

Public opinion generally failed to resonate with the no-war camp's emphasis on the question of US motives. Any concerns on this point seem to have been assuaged by the passing of UNSC resolution 678, which gave 'Iraq one final opportunity, a pause of goodwill' to withdraw from Kuwait on or before 15 January 1991. Failure to withdraw would result in the international community taking 'all necessary means to uphold and implement resolution 660 (1990) and all subsequent resolutions to restore international peace and security in the area'.[56]

Given that the Cold War had ended so recently, securing resolution 678 was an impressive achievement. This was the only time in the UN's history, other than the UNSC resolution on Korea in 1950, that the Security Council had authorized the use of military force.[57] Given the UN's past record there was some disagreement between the allies as to the desirability of going via the UN. Some countries, including the UK, suggested it would be wiser simply to rely on Article 51 of the UN Charter, which recognized the inherent right to self-defence. While this would have been legal, Bush thought a further UNSC resolution would help maintain the international coalition while also allaying domestic fears within the USA.[58]

The British Government's position was at odds with public opinion. Polls throughout the crisis clearly indicated that support for military action was dependent on securing UN authorization. Support for military action without UN backing fell to 30 per cent.[59] Although 49 per cent of the population were willing to support the use of force as soon as the UN deadline expired, 43 per cent were willing to give sanctions more time to work. Only 14 per cent of the latter group were unwilling to support the use of force under any circumstances.[60] Ironically, between 80 and 90 per cent thought the toppling of Saddam Hussein should be the war's primary objective.[61]

Securing resolution 678 maintained parliamentary support for the war. On 7 September 1990 the House of Commons voted by 437 to 35 in favour of UK participation in the international coalition. By 15 January 1991 political support had increased to 534 to 57 in favour. This unity was surprising given the impending General Election. While many Labour backbenchers remained concerned at the prospect of war, there was recognition within the Parliamentary Labour Party that Labour had to escape its traditional vulnerabilities on defence. In exchange for Labour's support Margaret Thatcher and her successor John Major refused to exploit Labour's divisions.

The issue of UN authority formed a central part of the debate within the churches. Writing before UNSC resolution 678, Philip Crowe observed that 'a clear mandate for offensive action against Iraq, provided by the UN Security Council under Article 42, is now essential if there is to be lawful authority for war'.[62] Cardinal Hume worried that military action without an additional UN Security Council resolution would 'undermine the unprecedented degree of international co-operation and trust which had emerged following the end of the cold war'.[63] Archbishop Runcie took the same view: 'For virtually the first time since its inception, the UN has acted as its founders intended. That is a triumph for international order, which should not be allowed to crumble.'

UNSC resolution 678 reassured many within the churches who had previously opposed the use of force to liberate Kuwait. The Church of England's House of Bishops, which, as we have seen, had been divided, now found a degree of unity – as is illustrated by its statement on 15 January 1991:

We believe that the UN Security Council resolution provides the proper framework for resolving the Gulf Crisis and we commend the British Government for its consistent support of these resolutions. We believe that one of the most important developments of the crisis so far has been the emergence of the UN as an instrument of collective security.

Working through the UN was therefore seen as an important step in realizing the post-Cold War aspiration of making the UN an instrument of international peace and security.

Operation Desert Storm

Operation Desert Storm consisted of a five-week aerial bombardment and a three-day land campaign. Statements made by politicians as well as military strategists, prior to the offensive, indicate there was a concerted effort to ensure proportionality and discrimination:

We do not seek the destruction of Iraq. We have respect for the Iraqi people, for the importance of Iraq in the region. We do not want a country so destabilised that Iraq itself could be a target for aggression.[64]

Military analysts also argued that even accidental civilian casualties would fuel Saddam's propaganda machinery.[65] Such statements gave the impression that the allies were engaged in a war with limited political objectives conducted with military precision in accordance with international laws governing the conduct of war, thereby reducing to a minimum civilian casualties, as well as damage to Iraq's infrastructure. However, it is worth looking at these statements again in the light of information and data that emerged during and after the war.

These assurances appeared to be supported by the release of video footage which showed the precision targeting of the allied air strikes. Perhaps the most abiding image of the Gulf War was of pictures of Tomahawk cruise missiles turning left and right down the streets of Baghdad. These images, backed up by TV panels of experts commenting on the latest Pentagon briefings as to the number of sorties run and bombs dropped, created the impression of a sanitized war. The Gulf War produced a plethora of aerial photography, fact sheets and still photographs. Unlike Donald McCullin's newsphotos from Vietnam, the Gulf War only produced shots taken from a distance. The bayonet engagements of Mount Tumbledown in the Falklands War were replaced by a computer-simulated, virtual-reality concept of war.

The allies used modern technology for propaganda purposes. There was a serious concern, among political and military leaders, that public opinion might turn against the war, as occurred during Vietnam. Paul Virilio suggests that the technological advances enabled the allies to control the flow of information about the war and that this helped to silence public criticism.[66] The Bishop of Oxford, among others, expressed unease at this manipulation.[67] For the most part, however, the public remained transfixed by the technicolour display of battle that dominated the media's coverage of the war.

Precision attacks were made on an assortment of Iraqi government and military targets. Supply routes and command centres were targeted, as were elements of the country's industrial infrastructure such as bridges and communications systems. The effect was to paralyse the country, so preventing Iraq from supplying food, water, fuel and ammunition to its troops in Kuwait and southern Iraq. There were, however, instances, such as the bombing of the Amiriya air-raid shelter in Baghdad on 13 February, which inflicted over 300 casualties, where precision bombing caused what came to be termed 'collateral damage'. This attack, like other military mishaps, was not the result of deliberate targeting, but the consequence of bad intelligence as well as Iraq's decisions to disperse military units in civilian areas.

While precision bombing played an important role in disrupting Iraq's ability to control its forces, not all the ordnance dropped during the aerial bombardment was precision guided. Of all ordnance used, 91.2 per cent conformed to old-style bombing methods – in essence like that used in the Second World War. There were 17,109 items of ordnance dropped or launched by US aircraft or navy vessels that were guided to their targets. This compares with 177,999 plain unguided bombs similar to those used during the Second World War. Out of a total of 71,627 tons of ordnance dropped during the First Gulf War, only 6,631 tons were precision guided. Of the 177,999 unguided bombs used during Operation

Desert Storm almost a third were of the cluster variety.[68] These scatter a large number of bomblets whose combined lethal effect extends over a much larger area than a conventional bomb.

Old-style aerial bombardments were used to attack troop positions in Kuwait. These tactics were ineffectual in inflicting military casualties, but they contributed to the significant number of desertions, approximately 11,500 in total.[69] This old-style method of bombing characterized what has become known as the 'turkey shoot' on the road to Basra, where retreating soldiers came under heavy fire on 27 February. This action caused consternation among some coalition countries and was arguably the reason why Bush suspended the military offensive action on 28 February.[70]

The 'turkey shoot' raises a number of ethical concerns, which require further scrutiny. Was this action necessary and proportionate? It needs to be remembered that this military action occurred before the formal ceasefire on 27 February. It therefore remained important to maintain the pressure on the Iraqi regime and to prevent retreating Iraqi troops from linking up with divisions of the Republican Guard based in southern Iraq. As US General McPeak argued, the alternative to attacking a retreating and disorganized army is 'to wait until he is stopped, dug in and prepared to receive the attack. It's a tough business, but our obligation is to our own people and to end the war quickly, in the most humane way possible.' Despite the impression given by the media coverage, most of the vehicles were empty, which suggests that the casualties could probably be measured in the hundreds rather than the thousands. So although the military action was not in fact disproportionate, these images conveyed by the media frenzy surrounding this incident undoubtedly had the effect of creating a negative public opinion.

After the war, the Pentagon stressed the efforts it had made to discriminate between targets.[71] The Pentagon confirmed General Schwarzkopf's observation that 'because of our interests in making sure civilians did not suffer unduly, we felt we had to leave some of the electrical power in effect, and we've done that'.[72] However, the Pentagon's report conflicts with a report by the UN Under-Secretary-General, Martti Ahtisaari, which stated that the 'near apocalyptic destruction' of Iraq's infrastructure had relegated Iraq to a 'pre-industrial age in which the means of modern life have been destroyed or rendered tenuous'.[73] Ahtisaari's findings, which were echoed by a number of NGO reports, have led some to question whether the just war criterion of proportionality and discrimination had much practical effect.[74]

The intense aerial bombardment made it possible for the allies to limit their land campaign to just three days. Only one incident caused public alarm during the land offensive and that was the bulldozing of Iraqi trenches on 24 February which led to countless Iraqi soldiers being buried alive. This was distasteful but it is doubtful whether it violated the laws of war. The intent was not to bury Iraqi soldiers but to clear a path through the minefield separating the two sides.

Reliable figures do not exist as to the number of military casualties incurred during the war. The total number of Iraqi soldiers killed in Operation Desert Storm has been estimated at between 10,000 and 100,000, and the number of wounded at between 85,000 and 300,000.[75] In contrast, the allied coalition suffered 466 fatalities and 350 wounded.[76]

Although none of the legal rules of law were violated during Operation Desert Storm, the glaring imbalance in the number of military deaths, the substantial damage to Iraq's infrastructure, and the use of cluster bombs all raise important ethical questions about the conduct of the war. As Adam Roberts writes:

> The enormous disproportion of military deaths does raise unusual questions, even if they are not narrowly legal ones. How long is it right to go on bombing an adversary's forces . . . before engaging them in direct combat, which at least gives them a reasonable chance to fight or surrender? Against large concentrations of Iraqi force, was it right to use fuel air explosives which soldiers might not have a chance to survive even if they are outside their vehicles? Is there not a moral danger lurking in the idea that a war might be almost cost free in human terms for one side? Above all, this coalition war raises an issue, which may recur in some collective military actions in the future: that in conflicts between forces representing the international community and an offending state, there must inevitably be a built-in inequality.[77]

Adam Roberts is right to ask questions about the morality of aspects of the military campaign, and the explanation for the gross disproportion in the casualties lies in the collective psychology of some of the coalition members.

The primary US concern during the war was to avoid a strategy of incrementalism, which could lead to a 'Vietnamization' of the situation.[78] Throughout the war General Colin Powell, Chairman of the Joint Chiefs of Staff, urged the President not to use military force in a slow and incremental way but to use maximum force to disorientate the enemy. Bush, on more than one occasion, said that military action would not be 'another Vietnam'.[79] From this perspective at least, it is possible that Operation Desert Storm represented a limited war fought without the proper limitations on means imposed by strategic necessity. It reflected the duality in US war aims: Iraq's eviction from Kuwait and the reduction in Iraq's military capacity.

Churches and the war

Operation Desert Storm led to an initial flurry of church statements as it began, and then silence. Church leaders were less concerned to offer profound theological analyses of the morality of the war, focusing their attention instead on providing pastoral support to the nation at large. This took such forms as offering support to families with relatives serving with the armed forces in the Gulf, and also to standing in solidarity with local British Muslim communities.[80] This was particularly important given the Government's policy of deportation and detention of some Iraqi families living in Britain.[81] The churches' reticence during the war did not however prevent those Christian organizations which had opposed the war from expressing concern at its conduct.

A number of church leaders issued personal statements on 17 January. All the statements expressed sorrow at the necessity of having to resort to military means, but only Dr Runcie went so far as to describe it as a just war. 'My first prayers are for our servicemen and women in the Gulf and their families. They deserve our support. The cause is just, I pray that minimum force will secure the liberation of Kuwait.'[82] The emphasis of many church commentators, including those who had previously been opposed to war, shifted towards issues of proportionality and discrimination. Cardinal Hume stated:

> It is tragic that all steps taken to avoid war have failed . . .
> We must hope and pray that the war will be swift with as few

10

casualties as possible. A special intention in our prayers at this time must be that the present conflict does not escalate into the human and environmental disaster it could so easily become. War is always a terrible tragedy and we must hope that all our prayers these last days will contribute to achieving a greater good, that is a true peace in the Gulf founded on justice.[83]

Hume's position contrasted with that of Pope John Paul II who appealed to President Bush and Saddam Hussein to 'immediately abandon this war that is unworthy of humanity'.

Some Christian peace organizations that had been active in opposing the war momentarily appeared to lose their voice. Others such as the Quakers issued statements condemning the war, regretting that 'all parties have missed the opportunity for a non-violent resolution of the conflict'. By maintaining their 'opposition to war as a means of settling of disputes', they argued that 'war is contrary to the spirit of Christ'. Central to many peace messages was the call on

all parties concerned to end armed hostilities and to begin the process of dialogue and negotiation. Only a just and comprehensive solution through the United Nations, in close consultation with Arab and other regional parties, can lead to the security to which all the people of the Middle East are entitled.[84]

On 18 February a number of Christian peace organizations including Pax Christi launched the 'Christian Coalition for Peace in the Gulf'. The Coalition called for the immediate cessation of hostilities and the start of negotiations on the basis of the UN resolutions. Other such organizations banded together to form the Gulf Crisis Working Group, comprising among others, Quaker Peace and Service, the National Peace Council, the United Nations Association and Campaign Against Arms Trade. The Gulf Crisis Working Group organized a mass lobby of Parliament on 21 February.

While the formation of these coalitions might suggest a degree of consensus, the lack of co-ordination between them meant that they failed to achieve any significant mobilization of civil society. For organizations such as Clergy Against Nuclear Arms (CANA), these peace movements did provide a convenient vehicle for political action in support of their convictions. The Revd Alan Race, CANA's

Secretary, wrote to CANA members urging them to participate in demonstrations against the war, like the one held in central London on 2 February.

> The official Church response has acquiesced, albeit with a 'heavy heart', in the support of the war. We need to witness to an alternative strategy, which is for an end to the war and the beginning of a peace process. We must give the lie to the belief that there is hardly any opposition.[85]

As with the anti-war demonstrations prior to the war, these marches failed to make much impact on the public, which according to opinion polls remained in favour of the war. As the Archbishop of York, the Most Revd John Habgood, pointed out, calling for a multilateral ceasefire 'conveniently ignored the fact that what negotiation was unable to achieve before the war was even less unlikely to be achieved when animosities had been deepened and passions inflamed'.[86]

The Christian peace camp's activities were fuelled by the concern that the UK and the USA would not use proportionate force. An ecumenical grouping consisting of Pax Christi and Christian CND produced a statement in late January, 'Just Conduct of the War in the Gulf?', arguing against the war. Several hundred people, including bishops, theologians and concerned individuals, signed this petition.[87] It urged the USA and the UK to reject the use of nuclear or chemical weapons even in retaliation to similar attacks by Iraq. In the field of conventional weaponry, it urged the USA and the UK to reject the use of fuel-air explosives or other such weaponry, including cluster bombs, because of the risks of indiscriminate and disproportionate killing. It argued that targeting population centres, oil wells or Iraq's national infrastructure would be illegitimate and illegal according to the rules of war.

These efforts helped to raise awareness of those questions, which are central to the just conduct of a war. However, the limitations on war reporting made it difficult for churches and other organizations to judge the morality of the war's conduct. Individual incidents such as the bombing of the Amiriya air-raid shelter provided occasional points of media focus, but it was impossible to gain a clear overall picture. As a result church leaders, such as the Archbishop of York, resisted pressures to decry the war effort.

To start a war is to accept the probability that things will be done that will strain conscience. If and when such things are done, that is a good reason for re-examining the way the war is being fought. But the moral and political justification for going to war in the first place is not fundamentally changed by occurrences that belong to war's very nature. If it was right to go to war, then – given the maintenance of control and restraint – the consequences of that decision have to be accepted, and the costs to participants have to be borne, if the last state is not to be worse than the first. To go to war against aggression, and then to withdraw from it when unpleasant things happen, is to give an open invitation to future aggressors.[88]

To those reluctant supporters of the war, the war was necessary to prevent the UN from being seen to fail.

The World Council of Churches

The unwillingness of many British religious leaders to contribute to public debates about the conduct of the war contrasts with the position taken by the World Council of Churches at its Assembly in Canberra in February 1991. Supporters of the current world ecumenical movement see these Assemblies as 'the most representative gathering of Church leaders and Christians which occurs'. Whether or not this is accepted, the Assemblies provide a useful insight into one type of ecumenical contribution to questions of war and peace.[89] War dominated the Canberra Assembly's agenda. The Assembly's final statement as well as amendments proposed by Professor Konrad Raiser and the Bishop of Bristol, the Rt Revd Barry Rogerson, deserve further consideration.

The proposed WCC *Draft Statement on the Gulf War, the Middle East and the Threat to World Peace* appears strangely reminiscent of a bad 1970s' Labour Party Conference composite motion. The statement built on the earlier comments of the WCC General Secretary, Emilio Castro, 'deploring the US Government's decision to initiate hostilities'.[90] It urged the UN to 'stop the war and to return to a strict application of non-violent sanctions without deadlines as a proven means of gaining the compliance of Iraq'. It called on 'both Iraq and the coalition forces led by the United States to cease fire immediately and to work for a negotiated settlement'. It appealed to Iraq to 'offer guarantees that it will comply with Security Council resolution 660 by withdrawing completely and unconditionally from the territory of Kuwait immediately upon cessation of hostilities'. Furthermore, 'external powers' were 'to withdraw all forces from the Middle East – except those required to perform a peace-keeping role under UN command'.

Rather than taking the opportunity provided by the Gulf War to recreate itself in the entirely new post-Cold War context, the WCC draft statement showed how detached and impoverished its theological thinking had become on the issue of war and peace. The statement contained little if any theological reasoning beyond reiterating that Christians are called to be peacemakers. Even if the WCC's intention was to adopt a pacifist position, the proposed statement lacked any clear theological exposition of pacifism. Instead the WCC fell back on what can be described as a 'tendentious and myopic reading of Middle Eastern politics, coupled with a hoary charge that it was American power that was most to be feared'.[91]

To call for a ceasefire before Iraq had withdrawn from Kuwait was seen by some as being politically irresponsible. The WCC appeared oblivious to the fact that the allied coalition was acting under the auspices of the UN and that use of military force constituted a case of law enforcement. Missing from the draft statement was any recognition that sanctions had failed or that military resistance to aggression is ever required. As the Revd James Rogers from the Church of Scotland asked: 'Is the WCC trying to occupy some high moral ground, which so far removes it from the real world that it will not be listened to in the real world?'[92]

During the debate two key recommendations were considered and voted on, the first by Professor Konrad Raiser, of the German EKD delegation, and the second by Bishop Barry Rogerson, of the Church of England delegation. Raiser's amendment called on churches 'to give up any theological and moral justification of the use of military power be it in war or through other forms of oppressive security systems and to become advocates of a just peace'.[93] This wording echoed the Seoul Final Document of the World Convocation on Justice, Peace and the Integrity of Creation. The Seoul Document urged churches and governments to work for peace 'through giving up any theological or other justification of the oppressive, threatening use of military power, be it in war or through other forms of oppressive security systems'.[94] Raiser argued that the amendment sought to shift the focus of ecumenical social ethics away from the rights and wrongs of war in general towards the ethics of peace.

Raiser's amendment was carried by 263 to 193 with 79 abstentions. In the space of a few minutes the WCC had committed itself not only to a pacifist position but a position contrary to the right of freedom of thought and speech. A number of African representatives realized somewhat belatedly that this amendment prohibited resisting oppression by force. This had been seen as a vital ingredient in the black struggle for liberation in Africa. Despite Raiser's reassurances that the context of his amendment referred to the actions of states not resistance to oppression by their citizens, the African contingent lobbied their cause sufficiently to rescind the amendment by 366 to 160. Showing solidarity with African brothers and sisters proved more persuasive than those theological arguments suggesting that the WCC's position was politically and ethically untenable.

In contrast, the Rogerson amendment sought to bring the WCC position closer to that of the Church of England.[95] Rogerson argued that while he wanted the air war to stop and the land war not to begin, this was dependent upon Iraqi behaviour – its prior withdrawal from Kuwait. Rogerson argued that the draft statement failed to take seriously the UN resolutions requiring Iraq to fulfil its UN obligations.

> We would call for a cease-fire – but, and with Anglicans there is always a 'but' – the cease-fire must be linked to the United Nation's resolutions and this implies a withdrawal from Kuwait. We believe this, in part because we would want to support the United Nations as an institution, even if it has not gone about its business in the right way. We believe that the United Nations is an important organisation and without it, international security is not best served.[96]

The amendment sought to delete that part of the resolution urging the UN to return 'to strict application of non-violent sanctions without deadlines as a proven means of gaining the compliance of Iraq'. In its place it simply called upon Iraq to 'withdraw completely and unconditionally from the territory of Kuwait'.

Rogerson sought to make the WCC's position consistent with

that of the UN. It was not however consistent with the line of thought presented by the Assembly paper. Janice Love, who spoke on behalf of the WCC's Public Issues Committee, urged the Assembly to reject the amendment on the grounds that it would fundamentally shift the emphasis within the resolution. It was feared that the amendment would leave open the interpretation that the WCC supported the continuation of the war. If Raiser's amendment took the Assembly too far to one extreme in opposing the very concept of war, Rogerson's amendment took the WCC Assembly to the opposing extreme by committing the WCC to support the war. A clear majority defeated Rogerson's amendment.

What is the outside observer to make of all of this? Three conclusions can be drawn. First, the events surrounding Raiser's proposal shows that what is acceptable in general is sometimes controversial when applied to a particular case study. Second, it was said that 'the rejection of the Rogerson position was a clear rejection by the most representative body of world Christianity of the proposal that this war was "justified" or "just"'.[97] Third, while the statement represents an important act of solidarity, the WCC's concern for peace lost sight of the possibility that sometimes peace with justice can only be achieved by means of war.

Peace: the elusive quest

The ceasefire agreement on 3 March 1991 formally drew the First Gulf War to a close. The coalition objectives had been secured: Iraq had been evicted from Kuwait, and the legitimate Government of Kuwait restored. The scale of the military victory suggested that Iraq's military capacity had been significantly reduced. On 3 April 1991 the UNSC passed resolution 687 which set out the terms of the ceasefire agreement and the steps which Iraq had to take before any final peace settlement. Iraq accepted the terms of UNSC resolution 687 on 10 April 1991.[98]

UNSC resolution 687 set out the terms of the ceasefire and laid down conditions for the lifting of sanctions. These included:

- recognition of Kuwait's territorial integrity and newly demarcated international borders with Kuwait;
- acceptance of a demilitarized zone with UN peacekeepers along the Iraq–Kuwait border;

- the monitoring and destruction of all chemical, biological and ballistic missile weapons and acceptance of a permanent ongoing monitoring programme managed by the United Nations;
- the monitored elimination of nuclear weapons materials and capabilities, supervised by the International Atomic Energy Agency (IAEA);
- the return of all stolen property from Kuwait;
- acceptance of war-damage liability and a compensation fund managed by the UN;
- repatriation of all Kuwaiti and third-party nationals;
- a pledge not to commit or support any act of international terrorism.

It soon became clear that despite its acceptance of UNSC resolution 687, Iraq was unwilling to comply fully with the resolution's provisions. Most controversy centred on the disarmament provisions. As a result, Iraq and the UN remained at loggerheads over both the interpretation and implementation of this resolution.

Iraq's non-compliance with the UN weapons inspectors, UNSCOM, and its refusal to acknowledge the integrity of Kuwait's borders, led on 13 January 1993 to US, French and British planes attacking air-defence systems in southern Iraq. Further sorties were conducted in southern Iraq on 17 January when cruise missiles destroyed a 'nuclear fabricating' plant near Baghdad. Governments justified the attack on the grounds that Iraq's actions constituted a breach of the ceasefire resolution, which consequently allowed the international community to take all necessary means as authorized under UNSC resolution 678 to restore international peace and security. No additional UNSC resolution was deemed necessary.

This approach set the pattern for most of the 1990s. Military action would bring Iraq temporarily back into compliance with its ceasefire obligations, until such time as the West felt further military action was necessary. Successive UNSC resolutions throughout the 1990s failed to resolve this cat-and-mouse game. After 13 years of sanctions the issue finally came to a head with the Second Gulf War in 2003.

Despite some post-war suggestions that it would have been better politically and morally if the allied coalition had marched on Baghdad, this option was never seriously considered. Not only would such action have contravened the limited political objectives prescribed by UNSC resolutions, it would have led to major divisions within the allied coalition as to the inviolability of national sovereignty. Invading Iraq raised huge logistical questions, which the USA was not prepared to shoulder, especially in a presidential election year. As Dick Cheney, the US Secretary of Defence, stated:

> If we'd gone to Baghdad and got rid of Saddam Hussein – assuming we could have found him – we'd have to put a lot of forces in and run him to ground some place. He would not have been easy to capture. Then you've got to put a new government in his place and then you're faced with the question of what kind of government are you going to establish in Iraq? Is it going to be a Kurdish government or a Shia government or a Sunni government? How many forces are you going to have to leave there to keep it propped up, how many casualties are you going to take through the course of this operation?[99]

For these reasons, the allied strategy focused on forcing Iraq to withdraw from Kuwait while inflicting considerable damage on the Iraqi military to the extent that it could be contained within its national borders.

There was widespread international expectation that the humiliating defeat suffered by Saddam Hussein would lead to his downfall. A change of regime might have improved Iraq's co-operation with the UN weapons inspectors so bringing closure. Instead the brutality with which Saddam Hussein squashed uprisings both in the south and north of the country led to a humanitarian crisis. This faced the international community with the difficult question of deciding when it is legitimate to intervene in the internal affairs of another nation state. The Security Council responded by passing resolution 688 calling on Iraq to end the repression of its civilian population and to allow international humanitarian organizations access to the country.[100]

The resolution expressly recognized that Article 2(7) of the UN Charter prohibited interference in the internal affairs of another state. The resolution did not authorize the use of force to help the Kurds or the Shi'ites. Despite the absence of any express authority from the Security Council, the USA, the UK and France forcibly intervened in Iraq by creating safe havens and no-fly zones in the north and the south of the country. All three countries argued that they were acting in support of UNSC resolution 688.[101] The British Government outlined its position:

> We believe that international intervention without the invitation of the country concerned can be justified in cases of extreme humanitarian need. This is why we were prepared to commit British forces to Operation Haven, mounted by the coalition in response to the refugee crisis involving the Iraqi Kurds. The deployment of these forces was entirely consistent with the objectives of SCR 688.[102]

According to one international expert this was the first time in the UN's history that a country had espoused the doctrine of humanitarian intervention.[103]

Public opinion was a key factor in propelling the international community to respond to the plight of the Shi'ites and the Kurds. The distressing pictures of Kurds fleeing to the snow-bound mountains of northern Iraq galvanized large sections of public opinion to lobby their governments to intervene. Having previously urged the UK and the USA to persist with sanctions, British churches now unanimously encouraged the Government to take a more proactive line.

> The governments that made up the coalition forces have a continuing moral responsibility to help win the peace. The political will and financial resources which made it possible to liberate Kuwait must now be found to provide humanitarian aid to the Kurd and Shi'a populations in Iraq.
>
> The appalling treatment by Saddam Hussein of his own people during the last few weeks is potentially of comparable international significance to his invasion of Kuwait. Arguments, therefore, based on the principle of non-interference in Iraq's internal affairs (article 2.7 of the UN Charter) are, in my view, of very limited validity. In the Charter itself they are superseded by 'threats to international peace and security', and resolution 688 recognised that the repression of civilians in Iraq is such a threat.[104]

While the majority of UK churches were reluctant to endorse the use of force to reverse Iraqi aggression in Kuwait, they pressed for aggressive humanitarian intervention in Iraq to relieve oppression.

Saddam Hussein's brutal handling of these insurrections reinforced Western perception that so long as Saddam Hussein remained in power, Iraq would pose a threat to international peace and security. Faced with the dilemma of wanting to put an end to Iraq's repressive policies without invading Iraq, the USA and the UK gave priority to the use of UN sanctions as a punitive tool of coercion. Douglas Hurd stated: 'Iraq cannot be expected to be re-admitted to the community of nations while it has a delinquent regime. Iraq needs a leadership, which will respect her commitments as a member of the United Nations and the Arab League.'[105] Bush also argued: 'We don't want to lift the sanctions as long as Saddam Hussein is in power.'[106] This was a controversial strategy. The UN Secretary General, Javier Perez de Cuellar, warned:

> As Secretary General, I cannot agree with measures that are aimed at overthrowing the government of a country which is a member of the United Nations . . . If the objective of pursuing sanctions is to topple the Iraqi regime, then I do not agree. I cannot agree.[107]

Yet so long as Iraq failed to comply with its ceasefire obligations the UK and the USA were entitled to press for sanctions to be maintained on security grounds.

Even as early as March 1991 there was growing concern at the humanitarian crisis being produced by sanctions. The UN Secretary General supported the tabling of a resolution by Yemen, Cuba, Ecuador, India and Zimbabwe calling for an easing of sanctions on humanitarian grounds. Although the permanent members of the Security Council rejected this, they agreed in 1994 to the establishment of the largest ever UN humanitarian aid effort in the form of the Oil for Food Programme. This programme was plagued by the tension between denying Iraq access to those goods which might enable it to rebuild its weapons of mass destruction, and providing for Iraq's humanitarian needs.

Throughout the 1990s the British churches played a significant role in raising public awareness as to the perceived humanitarian consequences of UN sanctions against Iraq. Although churches agreed that there was a crisis there was lack of consensus as to how it ought to be rectified. The tension between humanitarian and security considerations proved as vexing a problem for churches as it did for the UN. The Catholic Bishops' Conference of England and Wales, the Church of Scotland and the United Reformed Church all called for the comprehensive lifting of sanctions. In contrast the Church of England through Archbishop Carey and its General Synod pressed for sanctions to be refined so that they would target the ruling elite rather than the mass of the population.

The churches' concern at the perceived humanitarian effect of sanctions failed to persuade the UK and the USA that sanctions should be lifted – precisely because sanctions were seen as an effective way of deterring and containing Iraq. The churches' thinking on Iraq in the period 1990–2002 appears at times to have been determined more by the question of human suffering, whether caused by war or by sanctions, than by the geopolitical realities facing governments. It is not without irony, therefore, that when after 13 years of sanctions the UK and the USA sought to resolve Iraq's non-compliance with UNSC resolutions through unilateral military action, some churches opposed such action suggesting instead that governments should persist with the policy of containment – that is, with sanctions.

Conclusion

Was the First Gulf War a just war? The analysis presented here provides support for John Major's claim, on the eve of the war, that Operation Desert Storm conformed to the just war tradition. Although there is frequently a palpable sense of unease when politicians use quasi-religious language to justify or explain political decisions, the First Gulf War provided a clear case of a just war following the criteria set out in the traditional understanding of a just war.

Iraq's invasion of Kuwait was an evil which needed to be resisted. It broke the most fundamental of international laws. The military option was only pursued after all other options – sanctions and diplomacy – had failed. Sanctions and diplomacy were not prejudiced by the military build-up but rather by Saddam Hussein's unequivocal refusal to search for an escape route. Exhausting alternative methods of conflict resolution helped to isolate Iraq internationally. It also led to the inevitable political judgement that only military force would restore the status quo. This judgement was reflected in successive UNSC resolutions, most notably resolution 678 which provided the international community with the necessary authority to use military force.

The conduct of the war also appeared to have conformed to that international law relating to war. The First Gulf War was the first electronic war, where missiles were guided to their targets. Although no war is casualty-free, the use of such equipment meant that carpet bombing of civilian areas was never a feature of military strategy. The decision to use decisive force avoided a Vietnam-style quagmire. Despite the discrepancies in the number of military casualties between the two sides, the fears of many that the war would result in millions of casualties proved to be unfounded. However, the decision to use cluster bombs, which by their nature fail to distinguish between combatant and non-combatant, allied to the strategy of targeting Iraq's infrastructure, raised moral issues which were rightly the focus of much ethical reflection after the war.

While the international community was successful in evicting Iraq from Kuwait, the failure to hold Iraq accountable, either for its repressive policies against its own people or to the UN, meant Iraq remained an unresolved problem on the international agenda. While the war might have been just, the peace remained elusive. Rather then being free to turn their attention to the pressing problem of Europe and the dissolution of the USSR, the persistence of the 'Saddam problem' meant that Iraq remained on the international political agenda for the next 13 years. In the seeds of victory were sown the seeds for the Second Gulf War.

And yet despite the ease with which the First Gulf War met the just war criteria, churches were reluctant to reach a similar conclusion. The churches' confused and mixed response to the First Gulf War was indicative of a tension between a Christian realist and a Christian pacifist understanding of the just war tradition. By taking the issues of proportionality and last resort out of their natural theological context, a significant shift in balance and emphasis occurred within the just war tradition. This inversion of the just war tradition amounted to a form of functional pacifism best defined as 'just war pacifism'. Prioritization of 'last resort' echoed the claims of many Christian pacifists who argued that all alternative methods of conflict resolution needed to be tried before recourse to war. The abandonment of sanctions in favour of military action naturally raised the issue of right intent and the motives of those countries that used force against Iraq. As a result much of the churches' criticism of the Government's handling of the Gulf Crisis appeared to be veiled in a shroud of anti-Americanism.

The churches' approach to the Gulf War reflected their understanding of what war meant during the Cold War. Churches that had been such a key component of the peace movement in the 1980s were slow to react to the changed international environment following the collapse of the Berlin Wall. While all churches remained concerned throughout the crisis at the moves towards military action, vocal opposition to government policy and indeed to some church policy stemmed from those organizations which had provided the backbone to the churches' peace movement in the 1980s. Many of the theological fault lines and tensions that were evident in the churches' response to the war remained in evidence throughout the 1990s.

5 | **Victory without Triumph: The Second Gulf War, 2001–2003**

> The threat to Britain today is not that of my father's genera-
> tion. War between the big powers is unlikely. Europe is at
> peace. The Cold War is already a memory. But this new world
> faces a new threat: of disorder and chaos born either of brutal
> states like Iraq, armed with weapons of mass destruction; or of
> extreme groups. Both hate our way of life, our freedom, our
> democracy . . . But these changes and others that confront us
> . . . require a world of order and stability. Dictators like
> Saddam, terrorist groups like al-Qa'ida threaten the very
> existence of such a world.
>
> (Tony Blair, Address to the Nation, 20 March 2003)

If the First Gulf War gave rise to the 'new world order' then the
Second Gulf War gave it renewed shape and meaning. The First Gulf
War was conducted under the auspices of the United Nations,
involving the largest military coalition seen in military history, with
clearly defined political objectives: the reversal of Iraqi aggression.
Military action was only taken once other options had failed. In
contrast, the Second Gulf War amounted to unilateral pre-emptive
action taken by the USA and the UK, with the implied but not the
expressed authority of the UN, and without clearly defined political
objectives. Military action was seen to prejudice other methods of
conflict resolution, specifically the UN inspection process. If the
First Gulf War offered a model for the use of force in the new world
order, the Second Gulf War revealed all that is problematic in
making decisions about war.

Tensions between states, as they sought to reconcile their political
differences through the UN, generated an unprecedented degree of
public and political debate. From the streets of San Francisco to the
cities of Bangladesh, millions united to voice their opposition to the
war. This debate sheds light on competing judgements as to when it

is right and necessary to use force and the differing world-views underpinning these answers.

From the British perspective, the debate provides insights not only as to how various sections of society viewed the question of war, but also the competing visions of Britain's place in Europe and the wider world. The intensity of the British debate, which saw the largest public demonstrations in British political history and a succession of ministerial resignations, threatened the credibility and survival of the Government, suggesting that established norms and conventions were challenged by the war.

To some critics the Iraq war was an illegitimate act of aggression fought on a pretext, an elaborate deception designed to promote US imperial aspirations. Intelligence was either misused or made up and these critics concluded that Bush and Blair were as culpable as Saddam Hussein. The failure to secure a further UNSC resolution was evidence that the moral and political case for war had yet to be made. In the absence of UN authorization, Operation Iraqi Freedom was therefore seen as both immoral and illegal.

To others it was a just and necessary war and the justification for the action was overwhelming – Saddam Hussein's criminal behaviour over two decades and his contempt for international obligations shown by his accumulation and past use of weapons of mass destruction. Attempts to disarm Iraq, whether through sanctions, inspections, diplomacy or targeted military strikes, had all failed, suggesting there was little value in persisting further with UN inspectors. The legal basis for the war rested on the grounds of self-defence and the claim that Iraq's weapons of mass destruction contravened the 1991 ceasefire agreement.

Given this polarity of views and the widespread reliance by both sides on just war language, what role did the British churches, the guardians of the just war tradition, play in the debate which preceded the war? An analysis of the positions of different churches and their contribution to the political and public debate offers some helpful indications as to the role of religion within British society. What does the churches' role within this debate reveal as to church–society relations and church–state relations in the twenty-first century? How far were the responses of the churches to the war shaped by the ethical and political calculations associated with the just war approach?

September 11: a revision in US foreign policy

The Second Gulf War cannot be explained without recourse to the terrorist attacks of 11 September 2001. These attacks brought to an end that brief period in international politics commonly known as the 'post-Cold War settlement'. In its place emerged the 2002 US National Security Strategy. This amounted to the most comprehensive revision of US foreign policy, and in turn of international politics, since 1945. Analysts remain divided on whether this Strategy will prove workable. However, born out of the ashes of the World Trade Center, it provided the framework through which the USA reappraised its policy towards Iraq following 11 September.[1]

The Strategy's premise was the acknowledgement that 'the US possesses unprecedented and unequalled strength and influence in the world'. In order to maintain this hegemony the USA must commit itself to 'dissuading future military competition, deterring threats against US interests and decisively defeating any adversary if deterrence fails'.[2] The Strategy document went on to argue that 'the gravest danger lies at the crossroads of radicalism and technology' with terrorist organizations acquiring weapons of mass destruction from rogue regimes.[3] The USA would strive to enlist the support of the international community, but would 'not hesitate to act alone, if necessary, to exercise our right to self-defence by acting pre-emptively against such terrorists, to prevent them from doing harm'.[4] The Strategy gave reassurances that 'the US will not use force in all cases to pre-empt emerging threats, nor should nations use pre-emption as a pretext for aggression'. Rather, it should be used where a 'common assessment of the most dangerous threats exist'.[5] The USA would 'not seek to use its strength to press for unilateral advantage' but 'to create a balance of power that favours human freedom in which all nations and all societies can choose for themselves the rewards and challenges of political and economic liberty.'[6]

Throughout the summer of 2002 President Bush articulated many of the Strategy's themes when explaining US policy towards Iraq. He acknowledged that Iraq was not an imminent danger, but 'the history, the logic and the evidence' suggested that Iraq posed 'a grave and gathering danger' that legitimated an early solution.[7] This reflected the sense of urgency following 11 September to tackle head on new and emerging threats. To wait until Iraq possessed a nuclear weapon would mean that a 'line would be crossed' as 'Saddam

Hussein would be in a terrible position to blackmail anyone who opposes his aggression'.[8] While such an attack was not necessarily inevitable it was nonetheless possible, and because it was possible inaction was the 'riskiest strategy of all'.[9]

The key factor in US foreign policy to Iraq following 11 September was not the issue of weapons of mass destruction but the nature of the Iraqi regime itself.

> The threat from Iraq stands alone – because it gathers the most serious dangers of our age in one place . . . By its past and present action, by its technological capabilities, by the merciless nature of its regime, Iraq is unique . . . The fundamental problem with Iraq remains the nature of the regime itself, Saddam Hussein is a homicidal dictator who is addicted to weapons of mass destruction.[10]

This analysis assumed that traditional methods of containment and deterrence were ineffective in managing the risks posed by Iraq. In a joint White House press conference with Tony Blair on 31 January 2003, the President said:

> Prior to 11 September, we were discussing smart sanctions. We were trying to fashion a sanction policy that would make it more likely to be able to contain somebody like Saddam Hussein. After September 11, the doctrine of containment just doesn't hold any water, as far as I am concerned. The strategic vision of our country shifted dramatically, and it's shifted dramatically because we now recognise that oceans no longer protect us, that we're vulnerable to attack.[11]

The emphasis therefore shifted from containment to active disarmament. The international community had been 'more than patient' in emphasizing an array of tactics in its efforts to disarm Iraq.[12] Given the perceived threat posed by Iraq, and the failure to make any measurable progress towards its disarmament, the only remaining option was to disarm Iraq by force.

This logic affected the US evaluation of UNSC 1441. UNSC resolution 1441 provided Iraq 'one final opportunity to comply with its disarmament obligations under relevant resolutions of the Council', by authorizing Iraq to provide the United Nations Monitoring,

Verification and Inspection Commission (UNMOVIC) and the International Atomic Energy Agency (IAEA) with 'immediate, unimpeded unconditional and unrestricted access' to any location and to all officials that they might wish to interview.[13] Iraq was obliged to provide, within 30 days of the resolution, 'a currently accurate, full and complete declaration of all aspects of its programmes to develop chemical, biological, and nuclear weapons, ballistic missiles and other delivery systems'.[14] The resolution warned Iraq that failure to comply with these obligations would result in 'serious consequences'.[15]

Reports made by Dr Hans Blix, Chairman of UNMOVIC, confirmed that 'Iraq appears not to have come to a genuine acceptance – not even today – of the disarmament which was demanded of it and which it needs to carry out to win the confidence of the world and to live in peace.'[16] Iraq's 12,000-page declaration of its weapons of mass destruction programme was seen as being 'rich in volume but poor in detail'.[17] The declaration failed to clarify issues left unresolved by past UN reports. The discovery of 3,000 pages of documents relating to the laser enrichment of uranium, found in the home of an Iraqi scientist showed that while Iraq was co-operating on the process, it was not providing active co-operation on substance, which was 'indispensable' to complete the disarmament of Iraq.[18] As a result the inspections were turned into a game of 'catch as catch can'.[19] The discovery of several 122 mm chemical rocket warheads, allied to tests showing Iraq's Al Samoud 2 missiles contravened the permitted range of 150 km, was seen as the 'tip of a submerged iceberg'.[20]

Despite the progress made by UNMOVIC and the IAEA in identifying some prohibited equipment, the USA never seriously considered using the UN inspection model as a policy of containment. As Colin Powell said in a speech to the UNSC: 'Leaving Saddam Hussein in possession of weapons of mass destruction for a few more months or years is not an option, not in a post September 11 world.'[21] Instead Bush surmised that since the UN inspectors had been working for five months, Iraq must be engaged in 'a deliberate campaign to prevent any meaningful inspection work'.[22] Bush therefore determined that, since 'peaceful efforts to disarm the Iraq regime have failed again and again', it was necessary rather than 'drifting along toward tragedy' by persisting with the inspectors to 'set a course toward safety'.[23]

Throughout the crisis the USA made clear that, while it would strive to enlist the support of the international community, it would not hesitate to act alone if that was necessary to exercise its right to self-defence.[24] Bush stressed repeatedly that although it was desirable for the issue to be handled through the UN, 'the course of this nation does not depend on the decisions of others'.[25] The failure to secure an additional UN Security Council resolution explicitly authorizing the use of military force confirmed to Bush that the UN was 'irrelevant'.[26] On the eve of a vote in Parliament, authorizing the British participation in Operation Iraqi Freedom, the US Secretary of State, Donald Rumsfeld, noted that if need be the USA would go it alone.

The USA consistently argued that UN support was politically desirable but not legally necessary. Iraq's weapons of mass destruction contravened UNSC resolutions and threatened US security. Iraq's contravention of its 1991 ceasefire obligations constituted a breach of the peace and reactivated the authority provided by UNSC resolution 678 to use 'all necessary means' to restore the peace. This legal interpretation had provided the basis for military strikes against Iraq throughout the 1990s. It also had similarities with the legal justification put forward by NATO for its intervention in Kosovo. Given these precedents, Bush argued that 'this is not a question of authority. It is a question of will.'[27] Although Bush did not invoke Article 51 of the Charter, Iraq was seen as a threat to US security and as such 'the United States has the sovereign authority to use force in ensuring its own national security'. A Congressional Bill authorizing the use of force, on 10 October 2002, confirmed this authority.

What then was the peace for which the USA and its allies fought the Second Gulf War? Bush played on a traditional theme within US foreign policy – of the USA as the last best hope for humanity.

> The qualities of courage and compassion that we strive for in America also determine our conduct abroad. The American flag stands for more than power and our interests. Our founders dedicated this country to the cause of human dignity, the rights of every person, and the possibilities of every life. This conviction leads us into the world to help the afflicted, and defend the peace, and confound the designs of evil men.[28]

The war was portrayed as one of promoting law and order, freedom and democracy rather than any territorial self-aggrandizement. A statement issued by Bush, Blair and the Spanish Prime Minister, Jose Maria Aznar, on 16 March 2003, confirmed the territorial integrity of Iraq and the need to 'support the Iraqi people's aspirations for a representative government that upholds human rights and the rule of law as cornerstones of democracy'.[29]

The US National Security Strategy, and its application to Iraq, has similarities with George Weigel's use of just war theory. Chapter 3 set out Weigel's argument that the threat posed by rogue regimes meant that states need not wait until they are actually attacked before they have just cause to use military force. Where a threat was real and growing, pre-emptive action would not contravene the defence against aggression criterion in the concept of 'just cause' – indeed it would give it real purpose. The criterion of 'last resort' would also be satisfied where rogue regimes made plain their contempt for international law and where it could be shown that the threat was intensifying. This necessitated a revision of the Westphalian system. The UN system should not be able to protect rogue regimes by preventing other states from using force pre-emptively to deal with a rogue regime.

This strategy document shocked the US mainline denominations. A statement issued by the United States National Conference of Catholic Bishops (USNCCB) acknowledged the repellent nature of the Iraq regime and its need to destroy its weapons of mass destruction, but argued:

> Based on the facts that are known to us, we continue to find it difficult to justify the resort to war against Iraq, lacking clear and adequate evidence of an imminent attack of a grave nature. We fear that the resort to war, under present circumstances, and in the light of current public information, would not meet the strict conditions in Catholic teaching for overriding the strong presumption against the use of military force.[30]

To the USNCCB the *Catechism of the Catholic Church* restricted just cause to cases in 'which the damage inflicted by the aggressor on the nation or community of nations is lasting, grave and certain'.[31] The doctrine of pre-emption to tackle weapons of mass destruction and rogue behaviour was seen as illegitimately expanding traditional limits on just cause, prejudicing alternative methods of conflict resolution. Rather than resorting to war it urged the Administration to persist with a policy of containment and deterrence by effectively maintaining the military and political embargo on Iraq while developing a more effective non-proliferation regime.

These competing approaches to just war theory centred on the tension within the tradition between the presumption against the use of force and the right to self-defence. These tensions, reflected within the UN Charter, ensured that the ethical debate had wider political implications. The crucial question was whether the nexus of threats in a post-September 11 world necessitated a development of the just war theory. Did the changed security environment in which states now found themselves require them to change the rules which governed their approach to international relations? These questions provided the backdrop to divisions within Europe as to whether the war was 'self-evidently justified' or merely an illegal act of aggression against a sovereign state.[32]

Old versus new Europe

Many governments found the language used in the Strategy document quite unacceptable; its view of power and how it should be used smacked of US arrogance. For, central to the strategy was the USA's self-recognition as the world's sole remaining superpower. This position had been privately acknowledged following the end of the Cold War but never publicly stated. Furthermore while states had previously used anticipatory self-defence as justification for military action, they had always shied away from promoting it as a security doctrine, preferring instead to interpret broadly the right to self-defence as provided by Article 51 of the UN Charter.

The US National Security Strategy document in general and its application to Iraq in particular provoked a variety of contrasting reactions from European governments. On the one hand there was the outright opposition to unilateral pre-emptive action expressed by France, which was articulated by President Chirac as he emphasized the need for a multilateral solution compatible with the UN Charter. In contrast Tony Blair sought to shape US interest and policy through an approach which emphasized negotiation and dialogue, even if that meant eschewing the multilateral process. Both these approaches, reflective of differing world-views, were based on the recognition of the need to reconcile US supremacy with the interests of the wider international community.

One of the most important, but often overlooked, foreign policy speeches made by Blair during the Iraq crisis was his speech to the Foreign Office Conference on 7 January 2003. This statement, similar in significance to his 1999 Chicago speech at the time of the Kosovo war, set out the themes and priorities underpinning British foreign policy. The first priority was that 'we should remain the closest ally of the US, and as allies influence them to continue broadening their agenda'. This priority was justified on the grounds not only of 'shared values' but because 'it is massively in our self-interest to remain close allies', and 'to use this alliance to good effect'.[33]

> The price of British influence is not, as some would have it, that we have, obediently to do what the US asks. I would never commit British troops to a war I thought was wrong or un-necessary . . . But the price of influence is that we do not leave the US to face the tricky issues alone. By tricky, I mean the ones people wish weren't there, don't want to deal with, and, if I can put it a little pejoratively, know the US should confront, but want the luxury of criticising them for it.[34]

This priority meant that 'Europe should partner the US not be its rival' and to facilitate this process Britain 'should help to be a bridge between the US and Europe'. Rather than challenging the unipolar system by creating rival roles of power, Europe needed to work with the USA to ensure that 'global change is accompanied by stability rather than chaos'.[35]

Blair's acceptance of the unipolar world conflicted with the position taken by some other European states. In 1998 the French Foreign Minister, Hubert Vedrine, put the point starkly: 'We cannot accept a politically unipolar world and that is why we are fighting for a multipolar world.'[36] France saw Europe as a counterbalance to US political and military power. As the German Foreign Minister, Joschka Fischer, recognized, 'the core concept of Europe after 1945 was and still is a rejection of . . . the hegemonic ambitions of individual states'.[37] Not surprisingly, the US National Security Strategy which spoke openly of maintaining the unipolar world, while contradicting Article 2(4) of the UN Charter by claiming a right of pre-emption, caused considerable consternation. As the French Foreign Minister, Dominique de Villepin, told the UNSC on 19 March 2003: 'Make no mistake about it: the choice is indeed between two visions of the world' reflecting 'different relationships between law and force, between international legitimacy and the defence of national security interests'.

Both models had benefits and limitations. Blair claimed that his influence with the USA had led Bush to seek a multilateral solution to Iraq by seeking UNSC resolution 1441 as well as a subsequent UN resolution. Hemmed in by Bush's timetable for war and French intransigence, Blair found himself in the end going to war without a fresh UN mandate. In contrast, France claimed that it had upheld the UN Charter by avoiding any 'automaticity' for war within UNSC resolution 1441. However, France's intransigence and its unwillingness to consider the setting of a UN deadline amounted to diplomatic ankle biting. Ultimately, the Security Council's inability to prevent a war opposed by France exposed the reality of France's own diplomatic weakness and the impotence of the Security Council.

European tensions centred on the ethics and legality of pre-emptive military action. The question was not whether Iraq had to disarm, but rather the means by which this should be achieved. These tensions were evident in the European Council's statement on Iraq, on 17 February 2003.[38] The statement confirmed the centrality of the UN, but recognized that the role of cohesive diplomacy, itself contrary to the Charter, had played an essential role in securing Iraqi co-operation. The Council recognized that force should only be used as a last resort, but acknowledged that inspectors could not continue indefinitely, even though in the absence of an imminent threat from Iraq foreclosing on inspectors in favour of military action would still constitute an illegal act.

These tensions became all the more acute in the negotiations for a further UNSC resolution. Bush and Blair argued that it was essential to impose a deadline because reports by Hans Blix to the UNSC showed that Iraq had yet to accept the need for peaceful disarmament. As the Foreign Secretary stated:

> These briefings have confirmed our worst fears – that Iraq has no intention of relinquishing its WMDs, no intention of following the path of peaceful disarmament set out in Security Council resolution 1441. Instead of open admissions and

transparency, we have a charade, where a veneer of superficial co-operation masks wilful concealment.[39]

If Iraq met this deadline then all well and good, but if Iraq missed this deadline then it would prove beyond reasonable doubt that Iraq had no intention of disarming.

To France and other members on the Security Council deadline diplomacy seemed to represent an unnecessary rush to war, which would pre-empt other more peaceful options. Dominique de Villepin observed:

> You have to face the facts: everybody in the Security Council, not counting the three or four countries that decided to stick to the logic of ultimatum, nobody believed that a full chance was given to the inspectors. Nobody. That's why we have such a situation in the Council. And secondly, when everybody was listening to the inspectors' regular reports, we could all see that progress was being made. So you see, you have to take into account the fact that the awareness of the international community is very important. The military timetable was going faster than this awareness, than this conviction of the international community and of the Security Council.[40]

Rather than setting deadlines, France, Germany and Russia proposed to strengthen the inspection process 'until we've reached a dead end'.[41] They sought a more intrusive inspection system, including mobile units, aerial surveillance, all working towards a programme of action which prioritized key remaining tasks according to a rigorous timetable.[42]

From a just war perspective the proposals raised the question of the relationship between just cause and last resort. In his final report to the UNSC on 22 April 2003, Hans Blix said:

> While I have at no time suggested that the war was a foregone conclusion, I have stated my impressions that US patience with inspectors seemed to run out at about the same time as our Iraqi counterparts began to be proactive in proposing new investigations, supplying more explanations and names. I did not imply that there was any causal link. Had I looked for one,

I would have assumed that the accelerating Iraq activity was prompted by the feeling that time was running out.[43]

This would suggest that the decision to foreclose on the inspectors was premature. However, any Iraqi co-operation needs to be put in the context of the previous 13 years. Iraq's co-operation with UNSCOM during the 1990s was sporadic and temporary, and designed to create international division so enabling Iraq to retain its weapons of mass destruction. While Blix was therefore right to suggest that Iraq was co-operating, this co-operation was incremental rather than comprehensive. Iraq sought to ward off military action by dividing the international community rather than complying fully with its international obligations.

Calculations as to last resort cannot be divorced from political reality. The lack of political reality shown by some UNSC members deprived the international community of its unity and thus its ability to persuade Saddam Hussein to co-operate. This unity was crucial if coercive diplomacy was to be effective. The UK draft resolution would have maintained coercive diplomacy. While this might not have led to Iraq's peaceful disarmament, persisting with UN inspectors without any deadline would have meant standing down the US and UK military presence in the Gulf, so removing the credible threat of force which had led Iraq to accept UNSC 1441. In this respect France's behaviour came to be seen as unreasonable in the sense that it allowed its own self-interest, the promotion of a multipolar world, to interfere with more immediate security calculations.

The British churches: divided in their opposition to the war

Given this polarity of views, what insights did British churches bring to the political debate? An analysis of the positions taken by the churches shows that there was a groundswell of opinion against the war, but it also shows that churches approached the issue in quite different ways. The churches' approach to the Iraq war shows how they reached their ethical decisions about war and peace in particular as well as their wider understanding of international relations. Despite the perceived unity of the churches in their opposition to the Government's support of US policy on Iraq, it will be suggested that the divisions between churches at the time of the First Gulf War resurfaced during the Second Gulf War. These divisions were between those churches who, in certain circumstances, are willing to regard war as a legitimate instrument of policy and those which, even if they are not formally pacifist, have often come close to opposing war as a matter of principle.

For the most part British churches accepted the need for Iraq's disarmament. Statements made by the Church of England's House of Bishops in October 2002 and January 2003 and by the Methodist Church in August 2002 and March 2003 affirmed the Government's stated policy of disarming Iraq. Iraq's disregard of the UN and its authority – as expressed in relevant UNSC resolutions – was seen as the primary international political concern. Both churches saw UNSC resolution 687 as key resolutions and accepted, as did the Catholic Bishops' Conference of England and Wales, that UNSC resolution 1441 represented 'the legitimate expressions of the inter-national community's determination to disarm Iraq'.[44]

Unlike Bush's regime-centred analysis, British churches adopted a more legalistic approach to Iraq. Churches paid less attention to the nature of the Iraqi regime itself, preferring instead to stress that Iraq's flouting of its UN obligations threatened international peace and security. Church statements were therefore often prefaced by the acknowledgement that 'the regime of Saddam Hussein is not one we support'.[45] While churches acknowledged that 'the regime in Iraq has no moral validity', this did not convince them of the need to resolve this situation by military force. Regime change was seen as 'a matter for the Iraqi people to decide for themselves', and for states to claim for themselves this right would create a dangerous prece-dent.[46] Others questioned whether because of the destructiveness of warfare such regime change would benefit the Iraqi people.[47]

When Tony Blair sought to make a moral case for war, such as his speech to the Labour Party's Glasgow Conference on 15 February, churches intervened to warn him against using explicitly moral or religious language. Archbishop Williams, the new Archbishop of Canterbury, warned Blair and Bush 'to tone down their moral rhetoric in the drive to war with Iraq'.[48] The Archbishop went further by stating:

> There is no war that is holy and good in itself and to bring in the heavy artillery of a religious kind, to say that this is the only way of resisting evil, is something that has to be watched for.[49]

Not all church leaders or clergy necessarily agreed with the Archbishop. Mr Morrison, a former SAS Chaplain, compared military action in Iraq to 'a kind of ethical surgery' necessary 'to cut the cancer of a corrupt and murderous regime from the body of Iraq'.[50] A similarly tough line was taken by the Bishops of Chester and Rochester, the Rt Revd Peter Forster and the Rt Revd Michael Nazir-Ali, who argued that the regime's nature made military intervention necessary and desirable.[51]

Common to all church statements was the theme that Iraq did not pose an immediate and present danger, and that 'to undertake a preventative war against Iraq at this juncture would be to lower the threshold for war unacceptably'.[52] The publication of the Government's dossier in September 2002, setting out the case against Iraq, led the Catholic Bishops' Conference of Scotland to say that it shared the concerns of those who 'remained to be convinced that the evidence made available to date justified such action'.[53]

In spite of the similarities between these statements, churches showed a range of different understandings as to when the use of force would be justified. The Church of England's House of Bishops accepted that the just war tradition should not be narrowly interpreted but should permit anticipatory self-defence where attack looked imminent. The Bishop of Oxford, the Rt Revd Richard Harries, made clear when he spoke in the House of Lords that 'The Christian tradition has never confined the question of just cause purely to self-defence. If a threat is real, serious and immediate, there might indeed be a proper moral reason for pre-emptive action.'[54] The House of Bishops went further by implying that this right should extend to those circumstances where humanitarian disasters appeared imminent.[55] In a similar fashion the Roman Catholic Bishops spoke of avoiding war 'unless, in the face of a grave and imminent threat, there is no other possible means to avoid the just end of disarming Iraq'.[56] Both the Roman Catholics and the Anglicans drew a distinction between anticipatory self-defence and preventive action on the grounds that preventive action distorted the just war criteria of last resort and therefore raised questions as to the motives of those using force.

It was this commonality of positions which led Archbishop Rowan Williams and Cardinal Cormac Murphy-O'Connor to state that 'doubts still persist about the moral legitimacy . . . of a war against Iraq'.[57] The Catholic Theological Association of Great Britain argued that the absence of an imminent threat would mean that 'a pre-emptive war could not legitimately be claimed as a self defensive measure', with the result that any such action 'would amount to an act of state terrorism'. This distortion, it was argued, was easier to avoid when the threat of war looked imminent.[58]

The distinction between preventive and anticipatory self-defence was rejected by a number of other churches. The Quakers argued that 'unilateral action by any state against another is contrary to international law and is deeply damaging to the principles governing peaceful international relations'.[59] The United Reformed Church (URC) stressed that 'the UN Charter does not permit other sovereign states to act militarily towards another state unless that state itself first launches an armed attack'. From this perspective it was 'difficult to imagine' the legality of a UN resolution which would allow any nation and its allies to attack Iraq.[60]

Such a position seemed to imply that, regardless of any evidence showing Iraq intended to launch a chemical or biological strike against the USA or its allies, the USA would have to confine itself to using diplomatic and economic instruments, until such time as it was attacked. This argument failed to acknowledge that states have consistently used armed force, in flagrant violation of the Charter, to such an extent that the UN Charter's provisions in relation to the use of force have, in effect, become inoperable. Rather than recognizing that this history of violation has created its own customs and conventions, and that the old norms derived from the Charter have been replaced, or at least rendered unclear, some churches adopted a narrow interpretation of the UN Charter which further threatened the relevance that the UN was perceived to have in the contemporary world.

The Methodists and the Baptists took a position between these two poles by arguing that 'any steps involving military action against Iraq, which may be deemed necessary as a last resort, must be explicitly authorised by resolution of the UN Security Council'.[61] This attempted to get around the evident tensions, between the Charter's presumption against war and the right to self-defence, by ignoring the fact that any UNSC resolution explicitly authorizing the use of force against Iraq would invariably breach the Charter.

By emphasizing the distinction between 'explicit' and 'implicit' UN authorization, the Methodists and the Baptists pointed to an equally contentious debate prior to the Kosovo war, where NATO intervened only with the implicit authority of the UN. It is unclear what had led the Methodist Church to move in the space of five years from accepting 'implied' authority, as the basis for intervention in Kosovo, to insisting on the need for 'explicit' authority in relation to Iraq.

Churches rejected the US strategy of preventative war but they did so for different theological and political reasons. The lack of an imminent danger in the case of the Roman Catholics and the Anglicans and the lack of any act of aggression in the case of the Quakers and the URC meant that all churches placed a heavy emphasis on resolving this crisis through alternative mechanisms.

> We recognise that the moral alternative to military action cannot be inaction, passivity, appeasement or indifference. It is vital therefore that all sides in this crisis engage through the United Nations fully and urgently in a process, including continued weapons inspections, that could and should render the trauma and tragedy of war unnecessary.[62]

This became a consistent theme in church comments.

This view reflected the churches' belief that even if Iraqi co-operation was not forthcoming the inspection process would contain and deter Iraq. As the Bishop of Southwark, the Rt Revd Tom Butler, argued in the House of Lords:

> The policy of containment – sanctions, no fly zones and so on – has worked well enough for 12 years. As the dossier shows, that policy is certainly effective in preventing the development of a nuclear capability. It is too soon to judge that that policy might not continue to work.[63]

In the same debate the Bishop of Oxford said:

> Although the situation has obviously changed somewhat since the UN inspectors left, it has not, despite Saddam Hussein's efforts dramatically changed. It has not changed enough to justify the hugely dangerous critical threshold of military action.[64]

This line of reasoning held that for the Government to argue against a policy of containment when it had actively promoted this strategy for the past 12 years constituted an impressive policy failure. After all, in a letter to David Konstant, the Roman Catholic Bishop of Leeds, in November 2000, Peter Hain, the former Minister of State with responsibility for Iraq, wrote: 'Sanctions have not been counterproductive to the disarmament objective. On the contrary, sanctions have kept a brutal dictator contained for ten years and have blocked his access to equipment and parts to rebuild his WMD arsenal.'[65] Why, then, with sanctions still in place and the return of the UN inspectors to Iraq was the Government seeking a military solution?

In raising the question of containment churches left themselves open to the charge of double standards. Churches had after all campaigned against sanctions and the no-fly zones throughout the 1990s. Containment, as churches well knew, was not a cost-free solution. Churches appeared to suggest that it was better for Iraqis to continue to suffer the pain of sanctions which some had compared to a silent genocide than risk the horrors of a limited war. The Quakers for instance argued that 'no end justifies the killing, maiming and bereaving of innocent people who already suffer economic sanctions'.[66] The Church of Scotland, too, suggested that any intervention would only add to the suffering of the Iraqi people.[67]

The churches seemed unwilling even to consider the possibility that a quick military campaign might mean less loss of life than if the international community persisted with a policy of sanctions. Despite their acknowledgement of the morally odious nature of Saddam Hussein's regime, and their earlier recognition of the serious humanitarian fallout of sanctions, churches still argued that the evil caused by any armed conflict would be greater than the evil it sought to remove.

Some churches faced more of a problem than others in confronting this dilemma. In November 2000 the General Synod of the Church of England voted in favour of targeted sanctions.[68] The House of Bishops then argued that the international community should take steps to reverse the erosion of the UN sanctions regime by giving financial assistance to Iraq's neighbours and so encourage them to enforce the sanctions. In contrast the Catholic Bishops' Conference of England and Wales suggested that the lifting of comprehensive sanctions should be offered to Iraq as positive incentive to comply with the demands of the UNSC. This seemed to overlook the fact that this had been the UN's policy since 1991, and that it had proved less than successful.

The apparent absence of an imminent Iraqi threat led churches to argue that sufficient time existed to resolve the crisis peacefully. They remained reluctant to say how long the UN inspectors should be given, instead stressing that 'every possible opportunity should be taken (however unpromising the prospect) for negotiation, dialogue and persuasion'.[69] The fall-back position was invariably that only the UNSC could determine when all other options had been exhausted and that 'no state, however powerful, should be left as judge and jury'.[70]

Placing such emphasis on the UN did not resolve the question of how governments should act if the Security Council was incapable of forming such a judgement. For the Church of Scotland the lack of agreement was evidence that the USA and the UK had been unable to make a convincing case for war.[71] To others, however, the lack of agreement did not necessarily prohibit military action. As the Bishop of Rochester observed:

> It would be desirable, surely, to seek a UN mandate for any action, but if the Security Council produces irrefutable evidence of a material breach of its own resolutions but fails to act, national governments may judge that such a breach constituted a threat to their security and the region. They could then be justified in taking action.[72]

These different readings of the UN Charter, reflecting a restrictionist and counter-restrictionist interpretation, were indicative of competing understandings of the morality of war. It was the tension between the two that led some to argue that the war was 'morally wrong' and others, such as the Bishop of Hereford, the Rt Revd John Oliver, to argue that the war was the 'least morally repugnant option'.[73] The implication of the arguments adduced by the Bishops of Rochester and Hereford was that an action which is illegal by international standards may not necessarily be immoral.

Would the churches have supported the war if UN agreement had been forthcoming? It has already been shown that some churches would have found it difficult to recognize as morally well founded any resolution which legitimized an attack on Iraq. Archbishop Williams also at times refused to commit himself to supporting such a war on the grounds that 'Christians generally would hold that, unless other means of conflict resolution had been exhausted, it would be hard to justify any pre-emptive action.' Others, like the Anglican Bishop of Salisbury, believed that any resolution would lack moral authority because 'of attempts to cajole or bribe it [the UN] into rubber-stamping the decision of the powerful'.[74] Despite these reservations it is difficult to see how, after repeatedly pressing Blair and the USA to work through the UN, the churches could not have recognized, albeit reluctantly, the case for military action.

Divided not only on ethics but also on strategy

In responding to the fact of US hegemony in general and the particular questions posed by the Iraq crisis in particular, churches divided along the lines associated earlier in this chapter with the positions of Chirac and Blair. In essence, it could be said, the Church of England and the Catholic Bishops' Conference of England and Wales assumed the role of advising the Government. In contrast the Church of Scotland, and many of the Free Churches, adopted a Chiracian campaigning position as a means to mobilize their constituency against the war.

Throughout the crisis the Church of England sought to raise the ethical and moral concerns which needed to be addressed prior to military action. Archbishop Rowan Williams used this language in his inaugural press conference in October 2002. This same language characterized the House of Bishops' statement in January 2003.[75] The House of Bishops' October 2002 submission to the Foreign Affairs Committee's Inquiry on Iraq was seen as a contribution to the discussions rather than as a definitive position. The Church of England made a further two submissions to parliamentary inquiries, one on the humanitarian consequences of any war, and the second on the decision to go to war. Bishops used their position in the House of Lords to raise with Ministers a number of points arising from these submissions. As 'Lords Spiritual' the bishops in the House of Lords naturally seek to contribute a religious dimension to debates so their speeches tend to be thoughtful and reflective rather than campaigning in character.

Only the Catholic Bishops' Conference of England and Wales

adopted a similar role during the crisis. Although the Roman Catholic Church is not part of the British political establishment in the
traditional sense, it is in a strong position to engage directly with
Government because of its size and relationship with the Holy See.
The similarity in the approaches of the two churches resulted in sustained bilateral co-operation between the two. The Archbishops of
Canterbury and Westminster issued a joint statement on Iraq in
February 2003, while the Chairmen of the Catholic Bishops' Conference's International Department and the Church of England's Public
Affairs Unit had a meeting with the Foreign Secretary on 3 March
2003.

In adopting this stance, the two churches recognized that the
Prime Minister's own strategy of engaging with the USA had reaped
positive dividends. Archbishop Williams confirmed this approach in
October 2002:

> All my instincts are in terms of bridge-building in Europe and
> the Middle East, but as a good Augustinian Christian I'm very
> suspicious of my instincts. I have a sense that the worst thing
> that we can do is leave the United States to it. The extra-
> ordinary challenge we've got is of trying to engage the current
> United States' administration in a common discourse – I don't
> think we can quite back off from that. It is something I think
> the Prime Minister is trying to do. I have my questions about
> that, as you will be aware, but I think it's an important task,
> somehow, to be done.[76]

Part of the Roman Catholic and Anglican strategy was therefore to
encourage Blair in his strategy of constructive engagement with
Bush, in the hope that this would lead to a moderation in US policy.

The deliberations of the Church of England and its Roman
Catholic partner were heavily influenced by the just war tradition. It
is not surprising that, by using a tradition which emerged as a result
of dialogue between secular and religious authorities, the Roman
Catholics and Anglicans were drawn into a dialogue with the Government. As the Bishop of Oxford explained in the *Observer* in
August 2002:

> Political and military judgements are also moral judgements
> and moral judgements cannot be separated from an assess-

ment of the consequences of any proposed course of action. The main task of the churches at a time like this is to put forward and press these just war criteria, probing and testing whether or not they might be met. In the end political and military judgements have to be made and those who hold power have the awesome task of making them.[77]

This position held that political and military judgements cannot be divorced from moral judgements. The Anglican and Roman Catholic contribution in this case was to seek to ensure that moral considerations were not lost in the political calculus leading to war. This role did not prevent them from making their own judgements as to whether the criteria had been met. In many ways reaching such a judgement was a necessary precursor to any dialogue with the Government.

In contrast, the Church of Scotland, the URC, the Baptist Union of Great Britain and to a lesser degree the Methodist Church adopted a policy of clear opposition which was earlier associated with the approach adopted by President Chirac. The aim was to put pressure on the Government through mobilizing their constituency against the war. The Church of Scotland openly campaigned against the war by participating in numerous political rallies and by lobbying MPs to oppose the war. Although they wrote to the Prime Minister arguing their case, the open nature of this correspondence and the way it was circulated to congregations suggests that the purpose was to influence Blair less through persuasion and more by political mobilization. One Church of Scotland official noted:

> Unlike the Church of England and the Catholics we adopted a campaigning rather than an advisory role. Although at times we sought to use persuasion by writing to MPs and to the Prime Minister, this activity merely served to strengthen our campaign against the war. The Scottish churches played an important role in mobilising the 100,000 people who participated in the anti-war march in Glasgow in March. Our own Moderator was a frequent speaker at anti-war demonstrations.[78]

The Church of Scotland measured the success of its strategy by the number of people it could mobilize and their ability to create a groundswell movement of opinion, which, it was hoped, the Government would find irresistible.

The politicization of many churches reflects a growing process of political activism within society as more and more people lose confidence in the ability to influence the political process through traditional methods of representation. Declining turnouts at general and local elections contrast with mass campaigns such as the anti-poll tax marches, the activities of the Countryside Alliance and the fuel tax demonstrations. Churches have been part of this process as can be seen by the significant part they played in the Jubilee 2000 campaign.

A number of churches worked with the Stop the War Coalition prior to the war. For some churches the Coalition provided a means by which their voice could be heard. As one United Reformed Church official recalls:

> Our efforts at writing to the Prime Minister got us nowhere. When No 10 did bother to reply, their letters usually started with 'Dear Sir or Madam'. They couldn't even spell the name of our Church right. We found it a bit insulting, but we are accustomed to it. It's a question of size. We are a small church and probably in their eyes we are pretty insignificant. But it is also a class issue. British institutional life is governed by tradition, which means that some churches have better access to Government than others. We were seen as a marginal grouping and treated accordingly. We had to look at other ways to make our views known.[79]

Pursuing a campaigning role gave churches greater visibility and opportunity to make their views known and heard. By collaborating with others in the anti-war movement they made a strength out of their own weakness.

How does a campaigning strategy affect theology? The need to mobilize a constituency against the war necessitated the development of a simple and accessible message such as 'Stop the War', 'Say No to War', or 'Make Peace Not War'. It is difficult to see what theological reasoning other than pacifism informed such messages. These slogans provided little room for debate as to whether there might be circumstances in which war against Iraq would be acceptable. This political mobilization invariably led to the marginalization of the just war tradition. One Church of Scotland spokesman remarked:

> Although we are not a pacifist Church it is difficult to remember a time when we either supported a war or didn't actually oppose one. We didn't really make any extensive use of the just war tradition, but we did take from it the question of last resort.

An official of the Baptist Union of Great Britain echoed this sentiment: 'The just war tradition cut very little ice with us Baptists. It is not part of our Church teaching, and as such it didn't really help us a great deal in determining how we responded to the war.'[80]

This rejection of the just war tradition is not surprising. The use of the just war approach requires a process of continual evaluation as to those conditions which need to be met before it is legitimate to resort to force. The need for brief slogans with which to campaign may be inimical to continual reflection and revision. The success of campaigning, it could be argued, requires a process of conversion. It tends to hold that the sheer number of those engaged in a campaign provides sufficient legitimacy to validate a stated position. It is not necessarily dependent on the coherency of the case presented but rather on attracting numbers.

An initial assessment of Operation Iraqi Freedom

Numerous books will no doubt be written about the conduct of the war and they will have the benefit of information that is not yet available. Only a sliver of hindsight has been available in the construction of the initial assessment offered in this chapter.

Although the stated political objective was Iraq's disarmament, the increasingly apparent military objective was regime change. While Operation Desert Storm aimed to seize territory, Operation Iraqi Freedom avoided territorial acquisition and even pitched battles. Whereas the First Gulf War comprised a five-week aerial bombardment followed by a three-day land war, the Second Gulf War integrated the air and land offensives into a policy of 'shock and awe' lasting less than a month.

From a public relations perspective 'shock and awe' was seriously unhelpful. General Tommy Franks promised before the war that four times as many bombs would be dropped in the first days of the campaign as in the whole of Operation Desert Storm. This evoked memories of the bombing of Berlin and Dresden. The subtext to the media's coverage was that civilians were being targeted. The *Daily Telegraph*'s headline on 22 March for instance read 'Baghdad Blitz'. These images probably conflicted with the strategy's intention and execution since 'this would be one of the most tightly controlled and overseen targeting campaigns in history. Platoons if not battalions of lawyers were on station to ensure the legality of hitting virtually every fixed target.'[81]

While the aerial offensive of Baghdad on 20–21 March 'imposed overwhelming fear, terror and vulnerability' on the people of Baghdad, the offensive was directed at government buildings and other centres of political and military power.[82] The aerial offensive 'caused only very modest civilian casualties'.[83] There were certain incidents where bombs went astray, but it can be assumed that these were genuine mistakes since the deliberate targeting of non-combatants would have been contrary to the rules of war and the logic of 'shock and awe'.

'Shock and awe' depended on loosening the structures of government so encouraging the civilian population to rise up against Saddam Hussein. Rapid dominance was central to this strategy and emerged following discussions in the 1990s to find ways of using technological advances to achieve rapid military victory by 'affecting, influencing and controlling the will and perception of an adversary'.[84] The aim was to dominate the enemy but in a way that did not require half a million troops being sent into the theatre of operation for a campaign lasting six weeks or more.

It is difficult to know how consciously this strategy structured the war. The allied strategy sought to pressurize Baghdad through the strategic bombing of fixed political sites, while simultaneously invading from the south with the aim of reaching Baghdad as quickly as possible. Special forces inside Iraq seized crucial targets such as oil fields. 'Shock and awe' language prior to the campaign, allied to the unsuccessful decapitation strikes on the Iraqi President, aimed to pressurize Iraqi generals into capitulating without a fight.[85] While the coalition forces faced unexpected resistance from Saddam Hussein's Fedayeen guerrillas the strategy contributed to the demoralization of the Iraqi army. An abiding image of the war was of Iraqi soldiers fleeing their posts in their nightshirts as the US forces approached Baghdad.

'Shock and awe' contributed to the routing of the Iraqi army as well as the softening up of key targets, but it did not lead to the Iraqi army conceding without a fight. However, the difficulty faced by British troops in Basra was eased by the targeted, although unsuccessful strike on the Southern Commander, Ali Hassan al-Majid. Similarly, the occupation of Baghdad on 9 April occurred following a strike on a Baghdad restaurant after intelligence reports as to Saddam Hussein's location. The targeting of key people within the Ba'athist party contributed to a confused control and command system preventing the effective deployment of Iraqi troops.

The war's success rested on using effects-based targeting and network-centric warfare. According to the Director General of the Ministry of Defence's Joint Doctrine and Concepts Centre, 'effects based operations focus on actions and their influence on behaviour, i.e. stimulus and response, rather than on targets and attrition'. In contrast, network-centric warfare 'promises to deliver Shared Situational Awareness, a condition where force elements achieve a common or at least a consistent understanding, of both the strategic and operational level context and the prevailing tactical situation'.[86]

Central to this mode of warfare is the use of information technology to provide military strategists with real-time intelligence. Use of unmanned air vehicles, remote sensors and satellite imagery provided a more accurate battlefield image. It allowed military commanders to see the whole theatre of operation in a three-dimensional battlespace and enabled frontline soldiers to call in vast firepower from across the whole theatre of war.[87] While this system did not prevent the high proportion of casualties from 'friendly fire', it did enable the coalition forces to maximize their military capabilities.

Effects-based targeting meant that throughout the war the emphasis was on outcomes and not merely on destroying things, as with the First Gulf War. Operation Iraqi Freedom saw 41,404 sorties flown.[88] Of these, 20,732 sorties involved fighters and bombers and a further 7,681 sorties involved airlifts of troops and equipment to forward locations. In total 29,199 tons of munitions were dropped during the operation, of which 68 per cent were guided to their location – a significant improvement on Operation Desert Storm. Guided munitions were used against military command centres and supply routes, while unguided munitions were used against enemy troop positions.

As in the First Gulf War cluster bombs were used extensively. Although the number of cluster bombs used remains uncertain, Norman Lamb MP estimated that there were up to 17,000 unexploded British bomblets left in Iraq following the war. While the British Government saw cluster bombs as compatible with international law, many pressure groups and NGOs, such as Landmine Action, saw them as an aerial form of landmine which were responsible for unnecessary civilian deaths. It is perhaps disconcerting given their indiscriminate nature that the Armed Forces Minister, Adam Ingram, admitted that UK forces had used cluster bombs in urban areas. This statement conflicted with previous ministerial statements.[89]

What ethical questions are raised by 'shock and awe'? 'Shock and awe' aims to use overwhelming military and technological superiority to cause the complete collapse of a regime. It holds that it is possible 'to achieve a near bloodless war in terms of ground combat if one can find the right coercive levers and use them effectively'.[90] Any military strategy that can secure legitimate political objectives with the least damage and destruction is to be welcomed.

In contrast to technical violence designed to provide the means of securing an identified end, 'shock and awe' is an expressive form of violence sending a clear signal to one's opponents. The ethical implication of 'shock and awe' is therefore dependent on the message that is being conveyed.[91] It is possible that the strategy sent contradictory messages. As Bishop Andreas Abouna, the Chaldean Bishop of Baghdad, observed on 25 March: 'Iraqis don't think this is a war of liberation. At the beginning they did, but now, after the bombs, day and night it is just a war, not a war of liberation. They feel their country is being invaded.'[92]

'Shock and awe' raises a series of ethical questions. First, have technological advancements and the desire for a relatively bloodless victory led to remote military encounters absolving soldiers of any responsibility for their actions? US warfare is built around weapons systems that can be fired thousands of miles away from the front line but delivered with pinpoint accuracy. Although the computerization of modern warfare makes it possible to talk of the intelligent battlefield, computers can only solve the practical rather than the moral questions of war.[93]

Second, what are the motives driving this military revolution? While any military campaign should seek to minimize casualties and destruction, does this strategy suggest a desire to have military victory 'on the cheap'? This might not be such a problem in war, but it becomes an issue if it determines the nature of peacekeeping following war. 'Shock and awe' might have contributed to the military success of Operation Iraqi Freedom, but it prohibited a smooth transition to peacekeeping operations. The lack of appropriate troops on the ground, capable of maintaining law and order, highlighted a serious deficiency in the overall military strategy. In doing so it revealed a major contradiction in the policy: between needing to take strong coercive action against a state's apparatus and winning the hearts and minds of the civilian population. If the aim of war is peace then it remains imperative that military and political strategists develop a more integrated operation which resolves these tensions.

Churches and the war

How did the churches contribute to those ethical issues raised by the war? Having raised serious doubts about the decision to go to war, churches faced a dilemma as how best to contribute to the ethical debate about its conduct. A noticeable shift marked the churches' attitude to the war, in that attention shifted away from *jus ad bellum* to *jus in bello* considerations. Some journalists criticized this transition as indication that churches were backtracking on previously held views. By the end of the war some statements appeared to adopt a utilitarian approach, by implying that the speed with which the main fighting had been concluded and the limited casualties incurred on both sides somehow justified the war.

Few doubted that the coalition forces would win, but there was concern that the cost of the war would be disproportionate. Richard Harries therefore urged politicians and church leaders to 'refocus' their concerns on the war's prosecution. In doing so he took a pragmatic stance on the war itself: 'We should never be where we are now, but God is ceaselessly at work: making things better out of the mess we have made of things; constructing even in our destruction some good even out of evil.'[94] Similarly, Rowan Williams wrote to all Anglican Primates: 'Whatever the many and varied misgivings expressed, the military action now being undertaken may help to bring a more stable future for the whole region.'[95] All religious leaders called on 'God to grant wisdom, judgement and compassion to political and military leaders' to ensure this greater good.[96]

These statements hide varying degrees of criticism of the decision to use force. A statement issued by leaders of various faith communities in Britain acknowledged that 'war can only be a limited means to a limited end', while a joint statement by the Archbishops of York and Canterbury adopted a 'neutral tone', by warning that war presented 'dangerous new terrain with unpredictable consequences'.[97] The Cardinal took a more critical stance by declaring the war as 'wrong and evil'.[98]

Despite these criticisms, what insights did the churches raise as to the war's progress? Despite invoking the language of *jus in bello* very few statements were made in this area beyond some which called for discrimination and proportionality. There was little attempt to deal with the ethics of 'shock and awe'. The most that was offered were comments by Richard Harries who drew analogies with the Kosovo campaign.[99] In practice, church leaders offered little in the way of comment until the war's final day. On 19 April Cardinal Cormac Murphy-O'Connor stated:

> I cannot help but be pleased that the war seems to be finished a lot more quickly than we imagined. I must say that my heart goes out, not just to those who died, whom we pray for, but for the families of the soldiers who died, or the non-combatants, the Iraqis themselves.[100]

Richard Harries echoed this line:

> I still think there were better, less brutal ways of containing Saddam Hussein; but I have no doubt now that the victory has been won and relatively quickly; and that great numbers of Iraqi people will welcome the fact that the coalition forces are there. Every life lost is a sadness. But it is remarkable that a military operation like this should have resulted in so few casualties on this side.[101]

There was a danger that this response appeared to overlook the allies' use of cluster bombs, or individual incidents like the bombing of the Baghdad marketplace, each of which raised its own ethical questions.

The churches' apparent reticence contrasts with the position taken by aid agencies. Tearfund's Director wrote in the *Guardian*: 'Cluster bombs violate an underlying principle, that the distinction between belligerents and innocent civilians must be maintained. It is inconsistent to use cluster bombs in the fight to remove Iraq's chemical and biological weapons.'[102] The Directors of Action Aid, Oxfam, Save the Children Fund, CAFOD and Christian Aid wrote a similar letter to *The Times*. They claimed that the use of cluster bombs was 'indiscriminate and morally indefensible' and 'should be stopped immediately', because the 'mounting death toll . . . will inevitably cast a long shadow over the rebuilding of an already shattered Iraq'.[103]

Why were the churches so hesitant to make similar contributions during the war? The speed of the war and the piecemeal media coverage made it difficult even for well-informed political analysts to gain an overview of the whole operation. The immediacy of the war, however, hid the structural problems behind the churches' silence. These factors were most noticeable within the Church of England.

Even as early as the first days of the war the media were reporting that the Church of England had made a 'decisive shift of emphasis over the past few days to take account of the reality of the conflict'.[104] *The Times* reported:

> Dr Williams has decided to keep a low profile, making further statements only as events require it. He will not contribute to BBC Radio 4's *Thought for the Day* slot and has refused requests for interviews and articles. This has led to a concern among some Church insiders that he is not fulfilling the prophetic role that they hoped he would embrace.[105]

A subsequent editorial in *The Times* supported the Archbishop's silence:

> The Archbishop of Canterbury is in a delicate position. Everybody knows his anti-war views, but he heads an established Church, many of whose clergy are out in Kuwait. He has a certain duty, with war under way, not to demoralise those on the front line. Dr Williams seems to have recognised this obligation. Having declared his stance before the war broke out, he has decided to remain silent on it.[106]

Other journalists did not necessarily share this opinion. Paul Vallely criticised the Archbishop for remaining silent, juxtaposing the Archbishop's refusal to do 'Thought for the Day' with the thoughtful manner in which it was handled by the Chief Rabbi, Jonathan Sacks.[107]

The tone of many Anglican statements appears to suggest the Church placed a premium on providing pastoral support to the nation at large and those chaplains serving in the armed services. Rowan Williams wrote to all the chaplains in the armed services reassuring them that, despite the Church of England's pre-war position, the chaplains stood 'in a long and honourable tradition of Christians bearing witness to the love of Christ in hard and dangerous places'.[108] The Archbishops' Council issued pastoral guidelines to all dioceses and parishes similar to those issued at the time of Operation Desert Storm.[109] Emphasis was placed on developing interfaith positions, with an assurance that the 'conflict is neither about religion nor between religions', and support for the 'efforts being made in Britain to build a society in which different faith communities can flourish side by side in mutual respect'.[110]

A number of commentators questioned this strategy. The Revd Giles Fraser, Vicar of Putney and Lecturer in Philosophy at Wadham College, Oxford, observed:

> There is a difference between blessing the soldiers and blessing the battle itself, but it's a slender one. And it's a difference that will be lost on those who want to characterise this war as part of a broader war of Christian-America against Arab-Muslims.[111]

Fraser believed the toning down of the Church of England's prophetic voice during the war was indicative of the political compromises which establishment necessitates.

> Part of what has led to the neutering of Christian resistance to war is the spiritualising of religion itself. The settlement that Christianity has made with secular modernity has meant religion giving up its claim on the public realm. It is relegated to the private, a matter of individual conscience, and politics looks after the public . . . Christianity accepted the terms of this division because it was keen to piggyback on the power and prestige of the state. Yet the consequences of this

public/private settlement is that the public and political implication of Christ's call to love one's enemy is misread as senti-
mental benevolence . . . Evidently an unjust war condemned
by the Church puts these chaplains in an impossible position.
For all the important and caring work they do, how can their
presence not be read as anything other than tacit support for
the war? [112]

Whatever the validity of Fraser's argument, the Church of England's
record during the Second Gulf War would suggest that, contrary to
Anthony Harvey's belief, the Church of England's role as 'the
guardian and interpreters of a tradition of reflection on the morality'
of war did not 'transcend the opportunistic judgements of those
who exercise power'.[113]

As noted in previous chapters the just war tradition acknowledges
the possibility that a war might be just but that it may be fought
unjustly. In such cases those who wage the war have a responsibility
to modify the way the war is prosecuted. Similarly, the tradition
holds that if the cause is unjust the war remains immoral even if the
war is fought justly. In those circumstances those who wage war
must reconsider the original decision to go to war. While churches
cannot remove themselves from the environment in which governments make decisions about a war's conduct, neither can they
divorce themselves from their own previous judgements as to
whether the decision to go to war was correct.

The distance travelled by some religious leaders during the war is
therefore striking. This is best illustrated by the content of many of
the Easter sermons preached at the end of the war. The Bishop of
Peterborough, the Rt Revd Ian Cundy, appeared to compare the
post-war hope of Iraq to the resurrection: 'That is a process of
resurrection, of new life arising from the evils and brutalities of the
past. The dying of one regime must lead to a better future for Iraq
and the Middle East.'[114] War had become, like Christ's crucifixion, a
necessary process of purification out of which a new body politic
could be born. The war's success appeared to erase the churches'
own opposition to the war. For instance, Cardinal Cormac Murphy-
O'Connor's earlier statement that the war was 'wrong and evil' can
be compared with his statement of 22 April:

What I think is that now is the time for reflection. I think it would be precipitate for me to come out with a sudden decision as to whether the war was a just war or fulfilled the criteria for me. I think the consequences of this war are going to be with us for a long time.[115]

The *Financial Times* observed that while several church leaders in the run up to the war had raised moral objections to the Government's support of US military action, 'the tone and text of Easter sermons tomorrow are now broadly in line with ministerial statements'.[116]

The hundred-day peace

It is too early to give a considered judgement as to the sustainability of any post-conflict peace settlement. The political and economic implications of the conflict on the Middle East and the future political shape of Iraq remain unclear. Although it is difficult to draw firm conclusions, it is still possible to discern certain trends that emerged in the three months following the war. By comparing these trends to previous attempts at nation-building some firmer conclusions can be drawn as to the durability and justness of any subsequent peace in Iraq. In doing so it is important to analyse whether the policies promoted by the occupying forces promoted the international common good or a particularistic agenda reflective of their own interests.

A report by the Carnegie Endowment for International Peace in July 2002 examined the USA's past experiences of nation-building.[117] Of the more than 200 military interventions in which the USA has been involved, 8 per cent were labelled as nation-building exercises. Of the 16 attempts to create durable democratic regimes only 4 qualified as successes: Japan, Germany, Panama (1989) and Grenada (1983). In the other 11 cases democracy failed. The Carnegie report concluded that the success of nation-building is dependent on whether the exercise is conducted unilaterally or multilaterally. Of the 16 cases studied 12 were unilateral and of these 10 failed.

The Carnegie report compares these efforts to the multilateral experience. Haiti in 1994 and Afghanistan in 2001 were both authorized by the UN, while efforts at nation-building in post-war Germany and Japan were either carried out as part of a wider coalition or under the auspices of the coalition. Although Haiti has its own unique problems and while no verdict can yet be reached in the case of Afghanistan, the evidence suggests that multilateralism 'manages risk, while unilateralism invites it'.[118]

The scale of the problems and the risks involved in Iraq are distinctly different from those faced by the international community in 1945. While Germany and Japan were relatively homogenous and highly literate societies with sizeable middle classes, Iraq at the end of the Second Gulf War had an atomized and fragmented civil society with little democratic experience. After three wars and thirteen years of sanctions, Iraq was an impoverished country with high rates of illiteracy. Washington's lack of historical ties with and knowledge of Iraqi society compounded these problems.

Despite assurances that the UN would be given 'a vital role' in the creation of the Iraqi Government, Security Council resolution 1483 provided the UN with only a marginal role.[119] The UN was relegated to serve as a vehicle for humanitarian aid, international financial contributions towards reconstruction and as a political advisor to the Coalition Provisional Authority (CPA).[120] The US-led coalition, rather than the UN, retained the final say in the moves towards representative government in Iraq.

In the three months following the war, how successful was the unilateral process in managing the risks which have been noted? Competing pressures within Washington contributed to contradictory policy impulses creating institutional paralysis in Iraq. The failure to respond to local security needs and the subsequent difficulties in providing an environment conducive to reconstruction created a policy vacuum filled by tribal and religious elders. The jockeying for position meant that very few people from the mass of the population emerged who were willing to assist in the reconstruction efforts at a national level.[121]

The lack of a unified political vision imbued with any degree of legitimacy exacerbated the social and political instability in Iraq. The Bush Administration appeared torn between a long-term view of reconstructing Iraq, requiring a heavy military presence, and a short-term view of transferring power to an Iraqi interim authority as quickly as possible. Competition between the two strategies, each with its own logic, was indicative of a bureaucratic turf war between the US State Department and the Defence Department. While the Defence Department promoted Dr Ahmed Chalabi and other Iraqi exiles from the Iraqi National Congress, the State Department sought to develop more participatory models of government.

The lack of a coherent vision contributed to a sense of policy paralysis in Baghdad. This prevented the pursuit of more forthright policies from the outset. Discussions within Washington, and between Washington and other capitals, as to whether democracy should be imposed or whether the international community should merely secure the preconditions for democracy appeared somewhat academic flights in view of the reality on the ground.

Most noticeable in this respect was the growing lawlessness and unrest in Iraq. Daily attacks on UK and US service personnel in Baghdad and Basra and attacks on the country's infrastructure suggested that the war had moved into a 'disturbing new phase, a guerrilla, counter-insurgency phase'.[122] The lack of security hampered the humanitarian aid effort. The UN World Food Programme was forced temporarily to withdraw from the Al Hurriya warehouse in Baghdad in June following ongoing unrest and theft. UNICEF reported that looting had destroyed repairs to the Al Rustumiya water treatment plant. Aid agencies reported attacks on humanitarian convoys as well as on their employees.[123] These attacks have been in addition to the bombing of the UN headquarters in Iraq on 19 August 2003.

The difficulties faced by the Coalition Provisional Authority in restoring law and order, and the continuing difficulties it faced from pockets of armed resistance, revealed the limitations of a unilateral framework. However, the lack of a clear political vision and the absence of any political will to commit further troops to Iraq resulted in the USA lobbying various governments to provide peacekeepers.[124] The lack of a clear UN mandate for these operations prevented countries like India, Pakistan and France from committing troops. The Indian Foreign Ministers stated: 'Were there to be an explicit UN mandate . . . the Government of India could consider the deployment of our troops to Iraq.'[125]

Local religious and tribal clans were forced to rely on their own militias to maintain law and order. In many places, different groups of Iraqis took responsibility for security themselves, creating local security communities or police services and using peer pressure to deter looters and gangs. This contributed to the militarization of an already fractious country. Faced with such insecurity Kurdish parties refused to stand down their 80,000 militia, while SICRI, an Iranian-backed Shi'ite organization, relied on its Badr Brigade. Other sectarian groupings also emerged, like that organized by Muqtada al-Sadr in the Saddam City, now Sadr City, region of Baghdad. The USA contributed to this process by arming and financing the Iraqi National Congress's Free Iraqi Forces. Paradoxically, in the three months after the war, the USA worked with the Nuahidin al-Khalq, previously considered to be a terrorist organization, to act as security guards on the Kirkuk–Baghdad road.

America's reluctance to solve this capability-expectations gap suggested that 'the reconstruction of Iraq will de facto be undertaken, as in many countries, by the strong and the ruthless'.[126] The Coalition Provisional Authority's inability to provide even an elementary level of security in the three months following the war led many people, including church leaders, to question whether enough was done to bring peace with justice to Iraq.[127] This led many to argue for the UN to play a more pivotal role in Iraq. As in the 1920s, the wishes of the Iraqi people appear to be marginal to the considerations of the Great Powers. If the mistakes of the past are not to be repeated in the future then it might yet become necessary for the UN to play a more central role in Iraq.

The dodgy dossier: just cause revisited

A central element in the US and British Governments' justification for the war was the need to disarm Iraq of its weapons of mass destruction. The failure to unearth these immediately following the war led to a heated political debate as to whether the British Government manufactured the evidence presented to Parliament. Subsequent parliamentary inquiries have failed to resolve this issue.[128] While it is not the intention to document the claims and counter-claims made by competing political factions, the post-war debate has important implications for the use of just war theory.

The coalition's inability to substantiate its pre-war claims led the US and British Governments to modify their position after the war. Donald Rumsfeld expressed his hope that weapons of mass destruction would be found, but he did not rule out the possibility 'that Iraq decided they would destroy them prior to a conflict'.[129] The British Foreign Secretary appeared to backtrack further by saying that while there was 'no question' that Iraq's illegal arsenal certainly did exist, it was now 'not a crucially important' question.[130]

To Clare Short, the former International Development Secretary, these revisionist statements showed 'we were misled . . . we were deceived in the way it was done'.[131] Robin Cook argued that the war was fought on false premises, while Hans Blix suggested the failure meant the war was not justified.[132] The British Government's back-tracking led even the mild-mannered Andreas Whittam Smith, the First Church Estates Commissioner, to assert that 'the Iraq dossier was more or less a fraud perpetrated on the public by Downing Street'.[133]

The House of Commons Foreign Affairs Committee's inquiry concluded that while the September dossier 'was probably as complete and accurate as the Joint Intelligence Committee could make it, consistent with protecting sources', it nonetheless 'contained undue emphases for a document of its kind'.[134] The Government's Communications Unit was cleared of exerting undue influence on the dossier's contents.[135] However, the Committee criticized the Government for placing undue emphasis on single-source intelligence, but accepted that the 'limited access to human intelligence in Iraq' made it 'heavily reliant on US technical intelligence, on defectors and on exiles with an agenda of their own'.[136] It concluded that, on the basis of the evidence available at the time, the claims made in the September dossier were well founded.

From a just war perspective the debate highlights the tension between subjective and objective reasoning in relation to just cause. The more governments move away from the use of force in self-defence to the use of force as a preventative action the more subjective the reasoning is bound to become. Just as the *jus ad bellum* criterion of proportionality requires subjective judgements based on hypothetical projections, which may or may not be validated, so preventative action requires similar judgements. Was the Government right to base its decision to go to war on 'only limited access to reliable human intelligence'?[137] Does limited human intelligence provided by dubious sources constitute 'demonstrable and compelling evidence of the hostile intent and capability of a perceived aggressor'?[138]

It is difficult to draw conclusions as to how critically the Government scrutinized the intelligence. Taken on its own it probably does not constitute 'demonstrable and compelling evidence', but when seen in the context of the previous 13 years it is easy to see how the British Government reached such a judgement. Based on the limited intelligence available at the time and aware of Iraq's past behaviour, and its failure to comply with UNSC resolution 1441, the judgement made by the USA and the UK at the time that Iraq posed an emerging threat to international peace and security appears justified.

The debate – both before and after the event – about the Government's handling of the decision to go to war highlights all that is problematic with preventative military action. The Church of England's Public Affairs Unit noted:

> No matter what conclusions the various inquiries make as to the validity of the evidence presented to Parliament, and regardless of any future discovery of WMDs in Iraq, clearer guidelines need to be established concerning the use of pre-emptive military action. Such guidelines are important both for the credibility and authority of government and for public trust and confidence.[139]

As a result it urged the Government to develop similar guidelines to those that it had developed regarding humanitarian intervention at the time of the Kosovo crisis, to provide a framework for assessing the legitimacy of any proposed pre-emptive action in the future. 'The absence of such criteria contributed to the public's sense of unease about the motives and justification for the action taken against Iraq.'[140]

Conclusion

Was the Second Gulf War a just war? This chapter has argued that its justness depends not on whether Iraq's weapons of mass destruction are found, but on whether it is necessary 'to adapt the concept of imminent threat to the capabilities and objectives of today's adversaries'.[141] The answer to that question is in part dependent on how far the terrorist attacks of 11 September 2001 have altered the security environment in which governments make decisions on national security. Even if it is accepted that the trinity of rogue regimes, terrorism and weapons of mass destruction legitimates a doctrine of preventative action, this would not necessarily make the Second Gulf War a just war. Such a judgement depends on whether the conditions for preventative action were met.

Answers to these questions were at the time informed by reactions to the vision of a unipolar world promoted by the US National Security Strategy. Thomas Friedman argued in February 2003 that if only Bush had embraced Kyoto the French would have acquiesced in military action against Iraq.[142] The US refusal to endorse the Kyoto Treaty on climate change as well as the International Criminal Court, indicative of a growing unilateralism within US foreign policy, led to tensions within the Atlantic alliance that came to a head at the time of the Iraq war. Michael Glennon has suggested that if the French approach had been successful then 'it would have returned the world to multipolarity through supranationalism'.[143] The Second Gulf War was therefore synonymous with a realpolitik struggle between the states as to the type of world order that should shape a post-September 11 world.

If it is possible to move beyond the immediacy of events then it can be argued that the Second Gulf War brought to a head various trends that were becoming more evident following the end of the Cold War. Most noticeable in this respect has been the willingness of some states to move away from a restrictionist interpretation of the UN Charter. As the Second Gulf War showed, some states are more likely to use military force to relieve oppression and to uphold international norms and conventions. Iraq's failure to meet its UN obligations is a case in point. In this respect the use of force no longer conforms to nineteenth- or twentieth-century models of warfare.

State practice as to the use of force is now rarely compatible with the UN Charter. The failure of the post-1945 internationalist experiment to subject the use of force to the rules of law has quietly been eroded by state practice. This is not to imply that the UN is obsolete. From the time the UNSC agreed resolution 1441 to the time it negotiated resolution 1483 over forty other resolutions were considered. In the absence, however, of clearly accepted rules of state behaviour, the just war tradition will continue to remain important in assisting governments to reach decisions as to when it is necessary to use military force. Yet for the tradition to be relevant it needs to be sensitive to the changes in military technology as well as the new security threats that face governments.

Throughout the crisis it was possible to discern competing uses of the just war tradition. As the consequences of the Second Gulf War continue to reverberate throughout the international system, it is possible that the move away from positivism in international law – and as enshrined so clearly in the UN Charter – may lead to a reclaiming of a role for ethics within international relations. This would help governments to grapple with the dilemmas of how to respond to the changed security environment in which states now act. As suggested by previous chapters there are marked similarities between the pre-Westphalian system that confronted Hugo Grotius in the seventeenth century and the post-Westphalian system currently facing ethicists. The implications of these developments need to be thought through.

In addition to questions raised by the decision to go to war in Iraq, the war itself saw the application of effects-based targeting and network-centric warfare. This revolution in military affairs, indicative of what some envisage as the arrival of the intelligent battlefield, should make it far easier than has hitherto been the case to ensure proportionality and discrimination in the conduct of war. The Second Gulf War saw more extensive use of precision-guided weaponry than had been the case in the First Gulf War. It is to be hoped that such developments will eliminate the need to use cluster bombs.

While the fall of Saddam Hussein's regime occurred relatively quickly, the process of transferring authority and the creation of institutions capable of sustaining democratic life in Iraq has proved a more perilous and messy affair. While smart weapons and technological wizardry secured military victory within four weeks, they proved less effective and, at times, counterproductive in establishing order after military action.[144] Without UN cover US coercive diplomacy merely served to undermine the occupation's legitimacy, so fuelling resistance and resentment.

We have seen that the Second Gulf War challenged established norms regarding the morality of using armed force. It is therefore not surprising that the churches proved reluctant to support the opening of the Pandora's box represented by preventative action. However, while the churches' opposition to the war was unprecedented, a closer examination of the logic undergirding the positions of particular churches suggests more divergence than consensus as to when it is acceptable to use force. While a few churches focused their efforts on seeking to influence government policy though dialogue, the majority of churches lobbied the Government by encouraging their constituents to participate in mass demonstrations and marches.

The difference in emphasis that churches placed on church–state and church–society relations affected the churches' use of the just war tradition at the time of Second Gulf War. Those churches that developed an approach based on their relationship with wider civil society were more likely to overlook the logic of the just war tradition in favour of a more accessible just peace tradition. This contrasts with the strategy taken by the Church of England and the Catholic Bishops' Conference of England and Wales. Both used the just war tradition not only to reach their own conclusion as to the justness of the war, but also to structure a dialogue with Government on those issue that needed to be resolved prior to military action.

The competing church approaches to the Second Gulf War suggest a number of other issues which merit further examination. Is the move by some churches away from the just war tradition to a just peace tradition reflective of a quest for relevance in an increasingly secular society? Or is it indicative of faults within the just war tradition and the limitations of a strategy of political engagement? Whatever the answer to these questions, and regardless of whether the differing church strategies are ultimately sustainable, it is suggested that the divergence between churches both in terms of political strategy and theological analysis makes ecumenical co-operation at times of international crisis difficult, if not impossible.

6 | Postscript

To be a serious partner, Europe must take on and defeat the crass anti-Americanism that passes for its political discourse. What America must do is to show that this is a partnership built on persuasion not command. Then the other great nations of our world and the small will gather around in one place not many. And our understanding of this threat will become theirs. The United Nations can then become what it should be: an instrument of action as well as debate. The Security Council should be reformed. And we need to say clearly to the UN members: if you engage in the systematic and gross abuse of human rights, in defiance of the UN Charter, you cannot expect the same privileges as those that conform to it. It is not the coalition that determines the mission but the mission, the coalition. But let us start preferring a coalition and acting alone if we have to, not the other way round.

(Tony Blair, Speech to the US Congress, 18 July 2003)

The Cold War is a fading memory, despite the fact that the fall of the Berlin Wall and the collapse of the USSR occurred little over a decade and a half ago. These events brought to a close the short and violent twentieth century and promised in its place a golden age of peace and stability where history, through the triumph of liberal democracy and capitalism, had run its course.[1] And yet looking back over the turbulent events of the last 15 years it is possible to conclude that old certainties have given rise to new uncertainties that challenge orthodox understandings of state sovereignty. A major feature throughout this period has been the changing nature of the state and of state sovereignty in the conduct of international affairs. If the old rules governing state behaviour no longer seem particularly relevant, it is far from clear what the new rules are, or even who should draft and enforce them.

This book has sought to track these changes and to see how the end of the Cold War, and the subsequent growth of networks of worldwide interdependence, have impacted on the way that states use military force. Events in previously far-flung and remote places now have immediacy and an impact on the determination of Western policy and objectives. Military intervention is the most high-profile example of this inter-linkage. Understanding when, how and why such interventions occurred in Iraq enable conclusions to be drawn not only on inter-state relations but also on intra-state relations in a post-Cold War era.

Allied to this analysis has been the examination of the contribution made by British churches to the debate that marked government policy towards Iraq from 1990 to 2003. It studied the efforts made by British churches to make their theology of war and peace relevant to this changed international situation. It set out the diversity of Christian approaches to war and peace while showing how one of them, the just war tradition, has shaped the international laws of war as well as the rules determining when it is right and proper to use military force. That this tradition emerged and survived as a process of dialogue between religious and secular actors testifies to the contribution which Christian ethics has made to international affairs. Against this background the book has sought to ask not only whether the just war tradition can stand up to the new challenges of the new world order, but also what contribution the British churches have made to this process.

Disorder or order: the new US century

The Cold War superpower rivalry and the threat of nuclear holocaust have been replaced by the emergence of new concerns, including gross abuses of human rights, intra-state conflict, rogue regimes, terrorism and the proliferation of weapons of mass destruction. These concerns have challenged traditional conceptions of security. In addition to these 'hard' security issues there are also a number of 'soft', but no less threatening, risks, such as environmental degradation, climate change and poverty. States' management of this new risk environment has redefined the use of force.

States have historically used force for material or territorial gain. They are now, however, more likely to use force to relieve acute suffering and to broker and maintain peace in ethnic conflicts. The priority now accorded to human rights challenges previous certainties, such as the inviolability of the sovereign state, and gives rise to new uncertainties as to when such interventions are legal. A state's relationship with its people is no longer that state's exclusive preserve. Where states commit gross human rights abuses and contravene the accepted international norms and conventions governing state behaviour then international sanctions may follow.

This development has been accompanied by the emergence of a regime-centred analysis, which takes seriously the nature and character of a regime's behaviour both in relation to its own people and also to the wider international community. Where states with a history of repression and aggression seek weapons of mass destruction, the international community has shown a willingness to act pre-emptively. This regime-centred analysis has been accompanied, since 11 September 2001, by the tendency to demonize rogue states by dividing the world into non-negotiable spheres of 'good' and 'evil'. Rogue regimes are seen as irrational, beyond the pale, outside civilization. They can only be addressed through force. This rhetoric and its normative connotations can lead to 'an analytical cul-de-sac' that denies negotiation and compromise.[2]

Emerging conventions challenge the Westphalian state system, most obviously in the use of force contrary to the provisions of the UN Charter. The Charter, a reification of the Westphalian system, prohibits both interference in the internal affairs of another nation state and the use of force, unless in self-defence or if authorized by the Security Council. While in practice states have rarely conformed to the Charter, they have in the past invoked it in order to give their actions a degree of legitimacy.

The US National Security Strategy of 2002 and the subsequent war against Iraq pushed the Charter, and with it the multilateral process, to breaking point. By failing to authorize pre-emptive military action against Iraq, the UN was seen by the USA as having failed to face up to the new security environment. By acting unilaterally, the USA threatened to consign the UN to a footnote in history. The US Strategy was the public expression of an unspoken premise of US strategic planning following the Cold War, the USA's intent to remain the world's pre-eminent military power and to use this power to prevent other states from challenging its hegemony.

A number of commentators have argued that there are marked similarities between the US world-view before and after the ending of the Cold War.[3] George Bush's 'axis of evil' speech and the rhetoric of rogue regimes is reminiscent of Reagan's perception of communism as an 'Evil Empire'. Both cast the world into 'good' and 'evil' with the proviso that 'you are either with us or against us'.[4] As in the Cold War, military means are seen as the key asset with which to defend this line. Yet whereas in the Cold War US military power was partially checked by the military power of the USSR, no such balance of power exists in the post-Cold War era. The USA's military power has developed unchallenged.

Comparisons between the First and Second Gulf war provide an index of this development. Although the First Gulf War saw the first use of precision-guided weaponry, 82 per cent of the missiles dropped during the war were similar to those used in the Second World War. By the time of the Second Gulf War, 70 per cent of missiles were precision-guided. More remarkable has been the shift away from sequential military warfare to an integrated military strategy combining the simultaneous use of land and air power. The use of remote sensors and satellite imagery constitutes a revolution in military affairs. One commentator has observed that Germany conquered France, Netherlands and Belgium in 44 days, at a cost of 27,000 troops. The USA and Britain took only 26 days to conquer Iraq, 80 per cent the size of France, at a cost of 161 dead. Whereas the German blitzkrieg relied on a 3:1 advantage in terms of troop numbers, the US policy of 'shock and awe' faced a 3:1 disadvantage.[5]

The military revolution is far from complete. Most of the weapon systems used during the Second Gulf War are old varieties of military platforms used either in the Second World War or in Vietnam. As these systems are replaced and upgraded, and as further technological advancements occur, such as the miniaturization of computing, advances in robotics, and nanotechnology, the dividends to be reaped from network-centric and effects-based warfare will become more fully realized.

> Imagine a battlefield where the whole of the area occupied by the enemy is under sensor surveillance. From the air by unmanned air vehicles and from the ground by sensors that observe, listen and report all enemy movements in real time, directly to the headquarters involved in fighting the battle. In the longer term the sensors could identify the target, alert the fire support elements and where necessary direct the muni-

tions to their final destination. The next step in such as system would be sensors, that not only watch, listen and report but armed sensors that actually fight and engage enemy targets. The possibilities are endless and within 10 years this technology will become a reality. An intelligent battlefield is fast becoming a reality.[6]

This prediction should not be dismissed as *Boy's Own* thinking. It reflects the end point in the ongoing revolution in US military strategy. While this revolution will make it increasingly easy for the USA to deter its enemies, it will inevitably, given the discrepancies in defence spending between the USA and the rest of the world, make multinational interoperability difficult if not impossible in the future. It is notable that the United States Joint Vision 2020 makes almost no mention of its allies or coalition partners.[7]

It is difficult to predict how sustainable or achievable the US National Security Strategy will be. Will it mark a brief unipolar moment or the start of a unipolar era?[8] Traditional theories of international relations, such as realism, would suggest that nations respond to gross disparities in power by seeking alliances and treaties. It is possible, therefore, that a multipolar world might be restored either through the EU finding its political feet or by China's ability to gain some degree of peer competitor status, perhaps through a new Sino-Russian alliance. Both the EU and China have internal economic and political weaknesses that make this a distant rather than an immediate prospect.

Other theories, such as neo-liberalism, stress that the increasing interdependence of states will act to curtail the policy options available to governments. Joseph Nye observes that the paradox of US power is that although not since Rome has any nation had so much economic, cultural and military power, that power does not allow the USA to solve global problems without involving other nations. For many key issues – from international financial stability to drug smuggling, and global climate change to terrorism and poverty – military and economic power alone cannot ensure success. An overt dependence on hard power might actually prove counter-productive to these objectives.[9] This thesis suggests that as technology spreads and non-governmental organizations, ranging from transnational corporations to terrorists, increase their power, America will inevitably reorient itself towards the global community.

The ethical implications of international developments

The changing nature of the international system allied to the revolution in military affairs raises significant ethical dilemmas as to when it is appropriate to use military force. The emergence of new security threats has given rise to new interpretations of just cause, while a regime-centred analysis appears to legitimate preventive action. The growing imbalance between states and the shift away from the UN Charter raises concerns as to the motives of those states that are the most insistent that new rules be written. The overwhelming military superiority of the West in general and the USA in particular point to new ethical risks and challenges.

Policy-makers are once again turning to those rules and criteria embodied by the just war tradition to assess the ethical implications of their management of the new risk environment. Most marked has been Tony Blair's doctrine of humanitarian intervention developed at the time of the Kosovo war. However, the perceived need by the USA to 'adapt the concept of imminent threat to the capabilities and objectives of today's adversaries', has seen the just war criteria of just cause and last resort reinterpreted further. In the absence of clearly defined international rules and laws this reliance on the insights provided by the just war tradition may prove productive. The strength of the just war tradition is that it is dynamic rather than static.

Churches and Christian ethicists who have generally participated in such developments in the past, by bringing their own moral wisdom to bear, have proved to be reluctant participants in this exercise. The balance of evidence presented suggests that the British churches have failed, and are failing, to meet the challenges of changes in world history that have occurred following the end of the Cold War and 11 September. Some have discarded the just war tradition entirely while others have misrepresented the tradition as rigid and timeless. The end result is akin to a form of neo-pacifism, which does not commend itself easily to government and policy-makers. These static principles tend to be detached from a contextualized and nuanced analysis of what politicians are actually able to do given the constraints that they face. In all instances the British churches appear to place in the public domain arguments and recommendations that politicians can rarely, if ever, implement.

The explanation for this situation is both cultural and theological. Kagan argues that Europe's need to escape its bloody past has led to a new set of beliefs about conflict, power and threat, while at the same time the USA has evolved into the guarantor of the European order by dint of its might and global reach.[10] Europe, he suggests, has turned its back on traditional balance-of-power theories in favour of a world of laws and rules and transnational negotiation and co-operation. Whereas Europe has entered:

> a post historical paradise of peace and relative prosperity, the realisation of Immanuel Kant's 'perpetual peace', the United States remains mired in history, exercising power in an anarchic Hobbesian world where international laws and rules are unreliable, and where true security and the defence and promotion of a liberal order depend on the possession and use of military might. That is why on major strategic and international issues today, Americans are from Mars and Europeans are from Venus . . . When it comes to setting national priorities, determining threats, defining challenges and fashioning and implementing foreign and defence policies, the United States and Europe have parted ways.[11]

The apparent success of the post-1945 European experiment, allied to Europe's diminishing defence spending, has led European governments generally to favour the resolution of security issues through multilateral institutions with an emphasis on compromise and negotiation, rather than on confrontation. As a result, 'America's power and its willingness to exercise that power – unilaterally if necessary – constitute a threat to Europe's new sense of mission', the mission being 'transmission of the European miracle to the rest of the world'.[12]

The emergence of a postmodern, post-industrial society in Europe has led to a focus on welfare issues. This has seen a prioritization of soft rather than hard security issues, like climate change, in European foreign policies. The churches' agenda mirrors these concerns. Prior to the Second Gulf War, the United Reformed Church commented that 'the true axis of evil in our day is environmental degradation, pandemic poverty and a world awash with weapons'.[13] Many churches share this threat assessment and the resulting prioritization of policy objectives which flows from it. The contribution which churches make to international development is recognized by governments and development agencies alike. Clare Short, the former International Development Secretary, and Gordon Brown, the Chancellor of the Exchequer, have been regular visitors to church assemblies and general synods, where they have both stressed the Government's desire to enlist churches' support in combating world poverty.

The predominance of development issues over other foreign policy considerations has meant that churches have tended not to work on a theology of just war, preferring instead to work on a theology of just development. The churches' international agenda mirrors increasingly that of the development agencies like Christian Aid, CAFOD and Tearfund. Invariably, when Western governments do use military force some churches tend to approach the debate from a developmental perspective, focusing not so much on the question of just cause, but rather on questions of proportionality and discrimination.

The European experiment, with its emphasis on resolving conflict and historical animosities through negotiation and compromise has in turn given rise to a confidence that any conflict can be resolved through diplomacy and economic inducements. To argue otherwise is to question the validity of the European model. In both Gulf Wars it was shown that churches placed an overriding emphasis on last resort. If only governments would decide policy entirely on the basis of strict reason, the argument seemed to go, the irrationality of both wars could have been avoided. The question is not so much one of ends rather of means. Churches' insistence on exhausting other means appears to reflect wider European trends.

Europe stands as a monument to a rules-based transnational community. Europe's imperial mission is seen as one of persuading the rest of the world of the benefits of multilateralism. There is, as has been shown, an honourable tradition in Christian political thinking, which holds that the eradication of war is possible through the creation of a new international system. The UN Charter, which inspired 'to save succeeding generations from the scourge of war, which twice in our lifetime has brought untold sorrow to mankind', is seen as the most visible expression of the Christian hope that a better world through mutual co-operation is indeed possible.

All church statements during the First and Second Gulf Wars

stressed the centrality of the UN and its Charter. Deviations from the UN and its Charter by the promotion of doctrines that legitimate humanitarian intervention or unilateral preventative action were treated with suspicion. Rather than acknowledging that the old rules no longer appear relevant, and rather than negotiating new rules and conventions, churches have tended to emphasize the need to uphold the old order. In doing so their adherence to a rules-based international system has meant that at times the churches have tended to confuse that which is legal with that which is moral.

It is hardly surprising that churches have increasingly become dismayed by the development of US foreign policy. Bush's rejection of the Kyoto Protocol, his refusal to join the International Criminal Court and his questioning of the continued relevance of the UN are seen as threatening not only Europe's, but also the churches', civilizing mission. This despite the contribution the USA has made both to European and to international security over the last hundred years. It is difficult even now to imagine Europe not relying on US military might to resolve security crises that emerge on its own doorstep. And yet, the alienation of British churches from the US experiment, indicative of a wider European scepticism as to the utility of US power, has led to a rejection of what Reinhold Niebuhr once called the USA's 'responsibility' for 'solving the world problem'.[14]

Events since the end of the Cold War, the shrinkage of time and distance facilitated by globalization and the emergence of a new risk environment have led to a growing awareness that the rulebook needs to be rewritten. States, liberated from the restrictions of positivism contained within international law, are once again debating the ethics of war. There is a role here for the British churches. How they contribute to this debate will depend as much on whether they can escape the positivism contained within their own theological thinking as it will on their ability to take seriously the international shifts and schisms which are currently unfolding.

In earning the right to be heard, churches will need to recognize that despite the benefits of the European experiment, the realization of the Kingdom of God remains, as Niebuhr has suggested, an 'impossible possibility'. In order to make a contribution to the unfolding of the new international order churches must make use of existing traditions, however imperfect, in the knowledge that unprecedented circumstances require not just moral courage but also versatile and creative discussions about the ethics that govern the causes and conduct of warfare in the twenty-first century.

Notes

Chapter 1: Reflecting on War: Politics, Power and Religion in the New World Order

1 Alan Wilkinson, *Dissent or Conform? War, Peace and the English Churches, 1900–1945* (SCM Press, London, 1986); Alan Wilkinson, *The Church of England and the First World War* (SPCK, London, 1978).

2 William Temple, *Thoughts in War Time* (Macmillan, London, 1940); Kenneth Slack, *George Bell* (SCM Press, London, 1971).

3 Kenneth Vaux, *Ethics and the Gulf War: Religion, Rhetoric and Righteousness* (Westview Press, Oxford, 1992); Andrew Goddard, *When is War Justified?* (Grove Books, Cambridge, 2003).

4 Wilkinson, *Dissent or Conform*, pp. 318–19.

5 *House of Commons, Official Report*, 18 March 2003, col. 120.

6 Christopher Hill, *The Changing Politics of Foreign Policy* (Palgrave, Basingstoke, 2003), p. 12.

7 James Turner Johnston and George Weigel (eds.), *Just War and the Gulf War* (The Ethics and Public Policy Centre, Washington DC, 1991), p. 45.

8 Turner Johnston and Weigel (eds.), *Just War and the Gulf War*, p. 47.

9 Turner Johnston and Weigel (eds.), *Just War and the Gulf War*, p. 46.

10 Turner Johnston and Weigel (eds.), *Just War and the Gulf War*, p. 47.

11 Turner Johnston and Weigel (eds.), *Just War and the Gulf War*, p. 50.

12 *The Economist*, 21 December 2002, pp. 64–6.

13 David Martin, former Professor of Sociology at the London School of Economics, as quoted in Rupert Shortt, *Rowan Williams: An Introduction* (Darton, Longman and Todd, London, 2003), p. 116.

Chapter 2: War and the Ambiguity of Scripture

1 This question assumes that churches should be involved in politics. This assumption is disputed by such Christian anarchists as the

French lay theologian-socialist Jacques Ellul, who accepts the necessity of the state but rejects its legitimacy. Ellul's argument has a number of parallels with Christian pacifism, which will be explored later in this chapter. Jacques Ellul, *The Political Illusion* (Alfred A. Knopf, New York, 1967); Jacques Ellul, *Violence: Reflections from a Christian Perspective* (Seabury Press, New York, 1972).

2 Anthony Harvey, *By What Authority?* (SCM Press, London, 2001), p. 2.

3 Archbishop's Commission on Urban Priority Areas, *Faith in the City: A Call for Action by Church and Nation* (Church House Publishing, London, 1985); Council of Churches for Britain and Ireland, *Unemployment and the Future of Work: An Enquiry for the Churches* (CCBI, London, 1997).

4 John Habgood, *Confessions of a Conservative Liberal* (SPCK, London, 1988), p. 124.

5 Roland Bainton, *Christian Attitudes toward War and Peace: A Historical Survey and Critical Re-evaluation* (Hodder and Stoughton, London, 1961), pp. 112–33, 150–1.

6 Susan Niditch, *War in the Hebrew Bible: A Study in the Ethics of Violence* (Oxford University Press, Oxford, 1995), p. 6.

7 Niditch, *War in the Hebrew Bible*, pp. 103–4.

8 Anthony Harvey, *Demanding Peace: Christian Responses to War and Violence* (SCM Press, London, 1999), p. 35.

9 Alan Wilkinson, *Dissent or Conform? War, Peace and the English Churches 1900–1945* (SCM Press, London, 1986), pp. 26–9.

10 As quoted in Christopher Coker, *Empires in Conflict: The Growing Rift between Europe and the United States*, The Royal United Services Institute (RUSI), Whitehall Paper 58, 2003, p. 61.

11 Adrian Hastings, *A History of English Christianity 1920–1985* (Fount, London, 1987), p. 45.

12 Karen Rasmussen and Sharon Downey, 'Dialectical Disorientation in Vietnam War Films: Subversion of the Mythology of War', *Quarterly Journal of Speech*, Vol. 77, no. 2, p. 178. See also Linda Colley's reference to Richard Hofstader's 'Paranoid Style in American Politics', *Guardian*, G2, 29 July 2003, p. 8.

13 *State of the Union Address*, United Services Information Service, 29 January 1992, pp. 1–2.

14 *The Economist*, 2 February 2001, p. 13.

15 Bob Woodward, *Bush at War* (Simon and Schuster, New York, 2002), p. 94.

16 Tony Smith, *America's Mission: The United States and the Worldwide Struggle for Democracy in the Twentieth Century* (Princeton University Press, Princeton NJ, 1994), p. 5.

17 M. Light, 'Exporting Democracy' in Karen E. Smith and Margot Light (eds.), *Ethics and Foreign Policy* (Cambridge University Press, Cambridge, 2001), pp. 75–92.

18 Michael Ignatieff, 'Empire Lite', *Prospect*, February 2003, p. 40.

19 Michael Lienesch, *Redeeming America: Piety and Politics in the New Christian Right* (University of North Carolina Press, Chapel Hill, 1993), p. 10.

20 Robert Zwier, *Born Again Politics: The New Christian Right in America* (InterVarsity Press, Downers Grove, 1982).

21 As quoted by Lienesch, *Redeeming America*, p. 10.

22 Peter Marshall and David Manuel, *The Light and the Glory* (Fleming Revell Company, Old Tappan, 1977), pp. 22–3.

23 John Eindsmore, *God and Caesar: Biblical Faith and Political Action* (Crossway Books, Westchester, 1984), p. 50.

24 *Independent*, 21 February 2003, p. 15.

25 *The Economist*, 8 February 2003, p. 55.

26 *The Economist*, 21 December 2002, p. 66.

27 Hans J. Morgenthau, *Politics Among Nations* (Alfred A. Kopf, New York, 3rd edn, 1960).

28 David R. Maple, 'Realism, War and Peace' in Terry Nardine (ed.), *The Ethics of War and Peace: Religious and Secular Perspectives* (Princeton University Press, Princeton NJ, 1996), pp. 54–77, p. 55.

29 E. H. Carr, *The Twenty Years Crisis 1919–1939* (Macmillan, London, 2nd edn, 1981), p. 10.

30 Hans Rommen, 'Realism and Utopianism in World Affairs', *Review of Politics*, Vol. 6, 1944, pp. 193–215.

31 Morgenthau, *Politics Among Nations*, p. 10; Hans Morgenthau, *Scientific Man vs Power Politics* (University of Chicago Press, Chicago, 1946), p. 201; Hans Morgenthau, *Politics in the Twentieth Century* (University of Chicago Press, Chicago, 1962), p. 15.

32 As quoted in Michael Mazarr 'George W. Bush, Idealist', *International Affairs*, Vol. 79, 2003, pp. 503–22, p. 503.

33 *The National Security Strategy of the United States of America*, September 2002, p. 31.

34 *The National Security Strategy of the United States of America*, September 2002, p. 6.

35 Woodward, *Bush at War*.

36   Tim Reid, 'US Defence Spending to Top $500 billion by the End of the Decade', *The Times*, 1 February 2003, p. 23.

37   Normunds Kamergrauzis, 'The Persistence of Christian Realism: A Study of the Social Ethics of Ronald H. Preston', *Uppsala Studies in Social Ethics*, Vol. 27, 2001, pp. 45–6.

38   John Atherton (ed.), *Social Christianity: A Reader* (SPCK, London, 1994), p. 29.

39   Reinhold Niebuhr, *Christian Realism and Political Problems* (Charles Scribner's Sons, New York, 1953), p. 119.

40   Reinhold Niebuhr, 'The Good People of Britain', *Radical Religion*, Vol. 4, 1939, pp. 4–16, p. 7.

41   Reinhold Niebuhr, *Moral Man and Immoral Society: A Study in Ethics and Politics* (Charles Scribner's Sons, New York, 1932), p. ix.

42   Kamergrauzis, 'The Persistence of Christian Realism', p. 48.

43   Reinhold Niebuhr, *An Interpretation of Christian Ethics* (SCM Press, London, 1936), p. 49.

44   Niebuhr, *An Interpretation of Christian Ethics*, p. 118.

45   Niebuhr, *An Interpretation of Christian Ethics*, p.118.

46   Reinhold Niebuhr, 'The Hitler–Stalin Pact' in D. B. Robertson (ed.), *Love and Justice: Selections from the Shorter Writings of Reinhold Niebuhr* (John Knox Press, Louisville, 1957), p. 80.

47   Ernest Lefever, *Ethics and United States Foreign Policy* (Meridian Books, New York, 1957), p. 12.

48   Reinhold Niebuhr, *Structure of Nations and Empires* (Charles Scribner's Sons, New York, 1959), p. 277.

49   Colm McKeogh, *The Political Realism of Reinhold Niebuhr: A Pragmatic Approach to Just War* (Macmillan Press, London, 1997), p. 127.

50   Niebuhr, *Moral Man and Immoral Society*, p. 234.

51   McKeogh, *The Political Realism of Reinhold Niebuhr*, p. 2.

52   *The National Security Strategy of the United States of America*, September 2002, pp. 1–2.

53   *The National Security Strategy of the United States of America*, September 2002, p. 1.

54   Mazarr, 'George W. Bush, Idealist', p. 509.

55   Richard Harries (ed.), *Reinhold Niebuhr and the Issues of Our Time* (Mowbray, London, 1986), p. 1.

56   Foreign and Commonwealth Office, *Mission Statement for the Foreign and Commonwealth Office*, 1997, p. 5.

57   'British Foreign Policy', Opening Statement by the Foreign Secretary, Robin Cook, at a press conference on the Foreign and

Commonwealth Office's Mission Statement, London, *Daily Bulletin*, 12 May 1997, p. 2.

58 *Sun*, 4 June 1999, p. 1.

59 Tony Blair, 'Doctrine of the International Community', speech given to the Chicago Economic Club, Chicago, 22 April 1999, p. 3.

60 Archie Brown, *International Relations Theory: New Normative Approaches* (Harvester Wheatsheaf, Hemel Hempstead, 1992).

61 J. Philip Wogaman *Christian Perspectives on Politics* (Westminster John Knox Press, Louisville, 2000), p. 345.

62 R. John Elford, 'Christianity and War' in Robin Gill (ed.), *The Cambridge Companion to Christian Ethics* (Cambridge University Press, Cambridge, 2000), pp. 171–82, p. 74.

63 There are numerous categorizations of pacifism each entailing their own value systems. Peter Brock, a historian of pacifist movements in the USA, England and Europe, identifies five categories: vocational pacifism, eschatological pacifism, separational pacifism, integrational pacifism and goal-directed pacifism. For further explanation as to this and other typologies of pacifism, see Jenny Teichman, *Pacifism and the Just War: A Study in Applied Philosophy* (Basil Blackwell, Oxford, 1986), pp. 1–9.

64 John Yoder, *The Politics of Jesus* (Eerdmans, Grand Rapids, 1972).

65 Walter Wink, *Engaging the Powers* (Fortress Press, Minneapolis, 1992), p. 173.

66 Walter Wink, *The Powers That Be: Theology for a New Millennium* (Doubleday, New York, 1998), p. 144.

67 Bainton, *Christian Attitudes*, pp. 178–84.

68 Coker, *Empires in Conflict*, p. 41.

69 As quoted in Coker, *Empires in Conflict*, p. 48.

70 *Observer*, 7 April 2002, p. 16.

71 Robert Kagan, *Paradise and Power: America and Europe in the New World Order* (Atlantic Books, London, 2003).

72 G. E. M. Anscombe, 'Modern Moral Philosophy', *Philosophy*, Vol. 33, 1958, pp. 126–52.

73 Michael Brown (ed.), *The International Dimensions of Internal Conflict* (MIT Press, Cambridge MA, 1996).

74 John Paul Lederach, *Pacifism in Contemporary Conflict: A Christian Perspective*, paper presented at the United States Institute of Peace Symposium on Religious Perspectives on Pacifism, Washington DC, 28 July, 2002, pp. 11–12.

75 Cynthia Sampson, 'Religion and Peacebuilding' in William

Zartman (ed.), *Peacemaking in International Conflict: Methods and Techniques* (United States Institute of Peace, Washington DC, 1997), pp. 273–318, p. 276.

76 As quoted in Michael J. Glennon, 'Why the Security Council Failed', *Foreign Affairs*, May/June 2003, pp. 16–35, p. 23.

77 Giles Ecclestone, *The Church of England and Politics* (Church House Publishing, London, 1981), pp. 30–1.

78 Reinhold Niebuhr, *Christianity and Power Politics* (New York, Charles Scribner's Sons, 1940), pp. 1–32.

79 Thedore J. Koontz, 'Christian Non-Violence' in Nardine (ed.), *The Ethics of War and Peace*, pp. 169–96, p. 170.

80 Just as it is dangerous to read the Sermon on the Mount as a pacifist mandate for non-violent resistance, so too there are pitfalls in assuming that those texts which appear to sanction the use of force constitute an acceptance of violence. Stuart Brandon argues that Luke 22.38 proves that Jesus encouraged his disciples to take up arms in a revolutionary struggle against Rome. This argument has been dismissed by a number of reviewers who rightly argue that these swords were meant for self-defence while travelling. S. G. F. Brandon, *Jesus and the Zealots* (Charles Scribner's Sons, New York, 1967). See also the review by Morton Smith, 'Zealots and Sicarii, Their Origins and Relations', *Harvard Theological Review*, Vol. 64, 1971, pp. 1–19.

81 G. Kittel and G. Friedrich (eds.), *A Theological Dictionary of the New Testament* (Eerdmans, Grand Rapids, 1964–76).

82 Reinhold Niebuhr, 'Is Peace or Justice the Goal?', *World Tomorrow*, Vol. 15, 1932, pp. 274–96, p. 220.

83 Reinhold Niebuhr, as quoted by Richard W. Fox, *Reinhold Niebuhr: A Biography* (Pantheon, New York, 1985), p. 79.

84 John Macquarrie, *Principles of Christian Theology* (SCM Press, London, 1966), p. 13.

85 Harvey, *By What Authority?*, p. 11.

Chapter 3: Rediscovering the Just War Tradition

1 Gordon Zahn, 'An Infamous Victory', *Commonweal*, 1 June 1991, pp. 366–8, p. 366.

2 James Turner Johnston, *Morality and Contemporary Warfare* (Yale University Press, New Haven, 1999), p. 23.

3 Paul Ramsey, *War and Christian Conscience* (Duke University Press, Durham DC, 1961), p. 86.

4   Michael Walzer, *Just and Unjust Wars: A Moral Argument with Historical Illustrations* (HarperCollins, London, 1992).

5   Anthony Coates, *The Ethics of War* (Manchester University Press, Manchester, 1997), p. 155.

6   Anthony E. Harvey, *Demanding Peace: Christian Responses to War and Violence* (SCM Press, London, 1999), p. 57.

7   David Knowles (ed.), *The City of God*, tr. Henry Bettenson (Penguin, London, 1972).

8   Robin Gill, *A Textbook of Christian Ethics* (T & T Clark, Edinburgh, 1988), pp. 297–300.

9   It could be argued that there are certain parallels between the age of St Augustine and the secular age the Church now finds itself in. Augustine sought a Christian ethic transferable to the public sphere, which would mirror the growing acceptability of Christianity in society. European churches find themselves in a predominantly secular environment with the result that there are pressures on them to withdraw from the public sphere and seek renewal through a reconnection with the teachings of Jesus. Jenny Teichman notes: 'Pacifism is a characteristic form of "renewal" for Christianity. There are some indications that Christianity today, even in its most institutionalised forms, is returning to a kind of pacifism.' Jenny Teichman, *Pacifism and the Just War: A Study in Applied Philosophy* (Basil Blackwell, Oxford, 1986), p. 11.

10 Peter Dennis Bathory, *Political Theory as Public Confession: The Social and Political Thought of St Augustine of Hippo* (Transaction, New Brunswick NJ, 1981), p. 20.

11 Augustine's letters to Boniface, quoted in Robert J. Daly (ed.), *Christians and the Military: The Early Experience* (Fortress Press, Philadelphia, 1985), pp. 76–82.

12 Edward Welty, *A Handbook of Christian Social Ethics* (Nelson, Edinburgh, 1963), Vol. 2, p. 396.

13 Richard Regan, *Just War: Principles and Cases* (Catholic University of America Press, Washington DC, 1996), p. 18.

14 Walzer, *Just and Unjust Wars*, p. 53.

15 Joan D. Tooke, *The Just War in Aquinas and Grotius* (SPCK, London, 1965).

16 Coates, *The Ethics of War*, p. 150.

17 Hugo Grotius, *The Law of War and Peace* (Walter J. Black, Inc., Roslyn NY, 1949), Bk 1, Ch. 3, Sect. 7.

18 Grotius, *The Law of War and Peace*, Bk 1, Ch. 3, Sect. 5.

19   John Finnis, 'The Ethics of War and Peace in the Catholic Natural Law Tradition' in Terry Nardin (ed.), *The Ethics of War and Peace: Religious and Secular Perspectives* (Princeton University Press, Princeton NJ, 1996), pp. 15–39, p. 23.

20   United Nations Security Council Resolutions 82 (25 June 1950), and 678 (29 November 1990).

21   Regan, *Just War*, p. 84.

22   William O'Brien, *The Conduct of a Just and Limited War* (Praeger, New York, 1981), pp. 27–8.

23   Regan, *Just War*, p. 64.

24   John Courtney Murray, *We Hold These Truths* (Sheed and Ward, London, 1960), p. 261.

25   George Weigel, *Moral Clarity in a Time of War*, The Second Annual William E. Simon Lecture of the Ethics and Public Policy Centre (The Ethics and Public Policy Centre, Washington DC, 2003), p. 15.

26   Coates, *The Ethics of War*, p. 189.

27   Turner Johnston, *Morality and Contemporary Warfare*, p. 34.

28   Coates, *The Ethics of War*, p. 146.

29   Paul Ramsey, *The Just War: Force and Political Responsibility* (Charles Scribner's Sons, New York, 1968), p. 405.

30   The danger with this approach is that an improper emphasis upon just cause can lead to an easier recourse to war, which overshadows the need to restrain its prosecution. Coates argues: 'A one sided and exaggerated emphasis on just cause may generate a moral triumphalism and a moral enthusiasm for war that transform a just war into a holy or crusading war, and have more in common with the militarist tradition than they have with the just war tradition.' This suggests the need to take a holistic approach to the just war tradition rather than giving precedence to any one criterion at the expense of any of the others. See David Welch, *Justice and the Genesis of War* (Cambridge University Press, Cambridge, 1993), p. 34; Coates, *The Ethics of War*, p. 146.

31   Ramsey, *The Just War*, p. 152.

32   Christopher Coker, *Humane Warfare* (Routledge, London, 2001), p. 2.

33   Major Charles Heyman, 'The Intelligent Battlefield', Conference Paper to the Royal United Services Institute Seminar on Future Weaponry, London, 19 May 2003.

34   Coates, *The Ethics of War*, p. 170.

35   Weigel, *Moral Clarity in a Time of War*, p. 7.

36 Susan Niditch, *War in the Hebrew Bible: A Study in the Ethics of Violence* (Oxford University Press, Oxford, 1993), p. 155.
37 While this analysis starts with Grotius, it should be recognized that the rules governing armed conflict dating back to Greek and Roman times played an important role in shaping fundamental rules of the contemporary laws of war from the Middle Ages onwards. Coleman Phillipson, *The International Law and Custom of Ancient Greece and Rome* (Macmillan, London, 1911), Vol. II, pp. 166–384; Maurice Keen, *The Laws of War in the Late Middle Ages* (Routledge, London, 1965).
38 Adam Roberts and Richard Guelff, *Documents on the Laws of War* (Oxford University Press, Oxford, 2001), pp. 47–138.
39 Roberts and Guelff, *Documents on the Laws of War*, pp. 155–68.
40 Roberts and Guelff, *Documents on the Laws of War*, pp. 419–512.
41 Coker, *Humane Warfare*.
42 Hugo Slim, 'Why Protect Civilians', *International Affairs*, Vol. 79, 2003, pp. 481–502, p. 487.
43 Brian Rodley, 'After Bangladesh: The Law of Humanitarian Intervention by Military Force', *Journal of International Law*, 1973, pp. 271–83, p. 275.
44 As quoted in Christine Gray, *International Law and the Use of Force* (Oxford University Press, Oxford, 2000), p. 25.
45 As quoted in Gray, *International Law*, p. 30.
46 S/PV 3988 (1999), 12–13 (China), 13 (Russia).
47 United Nations Security Council Resolutions 1160 (1998), 1199 (1998) and 1203 (1998).
48 S/PV 3937 (1998), 15 (USA).
49 *Legality of Use of Force Case (Provisional Measures)* (ICJ, 1999), Pleadings of Belgium, 10 May 1999, CR 899/15.
50 *Legality of Use of Force Case (Provisional Measures)* (ICJ, 1999), Order of 2 June 1999.
51 Simon Chayes, 'Law and the Quarantine of Cuba', *Foreign Affairs*, Vol. 41, 1963, pp. 546–59, p. 550.
52 Gray, *International Law*, p. 112.
53 *United Nations Year Book* (1981), p. 275. S/14510.
54 Gray, *International Law*, p. 115.
55 SC 2288th meeting, para. 156.
56 *Guardian*, 5 March 1999, p. 1.
57 United Nations Security Council Resolution 262 (1968).
58 Anthony Arend and Robert Beck (eds), *International Law and the Use*

of Force: Beyond the UN Charter Paradigm (Routledge, London, 1993).

59   The USA reported its actions to the Security Council in S/17990; Security Council Debates S/PV 2677, 2679 and 2680.

60   'UK Materials on International Law', *British Yearbook of International Law*, Vol. 57, 1986, p. 641.

61   Gray, *International Law*, p. 118.

62   *Independent*, 16 July 1993, p. 12.

63   Regan, *Just War*, p. 20.

64   Hugo Grotius, *De Jure Belli ac Pacis Libri Tres* (1646), tr. Kelsey, Classics of International Law (Clarendon Press, Oxford, 1925).

65   Grotius, *De Jure Belli*, Bk II, 40.

66   Coates, *The Ethics of War*, p. 156.

67   St Ambrose, *De Officiis*, I.xxxvi.179.

68   As quoted by Simon Chesterman, *Just War or Just Peace: Humanitarian Intervention and International Law* (Oxford University Press, Oxford, 2001), p. 14.

69   As quoted by Chesterman, *Just War or Just Peace*, p. 15.

70   As quoted by Chesterman, *Just War or Just Peace*, p. 17.

71   Ian Brownlie, 'Thoughts on Kind-Hearted Gunmen' in Richard Lillich (ed.), *Humanitarian Intervention and the United Nations* (University Press of Virginia, Charlottesville, 1973), p. 139.

72   Tony Blair, 'Doctrine of the International Community', speech given to the Chicago Economic Club, Chicago, 22 April 1999, p. 3.

73   Chesterman, *Just War or Just Peace*, p. 66.

74   *The National Security Strategy of the United States of America*, September 2002, p. 2.

75   Weigel, *Moral Clarity in a Time of War*, p. 11.

76   Weigel, *Moral Clarity in a Time of War*, p. 13.

77   Regan, *Just War*, pp. 51–2.

78   Regan, *Just War*, p. 54.

79   Weigel, *Moral Clarity in a Time of War*, p. 11.

80   Weigel, *Moral Clarity in a Time of War*, p. 12.

81   Weigel, *Moral Clarity in a Time of War*, p. 14.

82   Weigel, *Moral Clarity in a Time of War*, p. 14.

83   Regan, *Just War*, p. 52.

84   Weigel, *Moral Clarity in a Time of War*, p. 15.

85   Vitoria as quoted by Bruce Hamiliton, *Political Thought in Sixteenth Century Spain* (Clarendon Press, Oxford, 1963), p. 105.

Chapter 4: Triumph without Victory: The First Gulf War, 1990–1991

1 President George Bush, *State of the Union Address*, United States Information Service, 29 January 1991.

2 *House of Commons, Official Report*, 15 January 1991, col. 721.

3 These comments were made by the Revd Philip Crowe in 'Thought for the Day', on BBC Radio 4's *Today* programme, 16 November 1991. They were subsequently reported in the *Independent*, 18 November 1990, p. 6, and in the *Sunday Telegraph*, 11 November 1990, p. 3.

4 *Guardian*, 1 November 1990, p. 6.

5 Keith Jenkins; 'The Story of an Era' in *Values, Challenges, Hopes: Brussels 1990–2002* (CEC, Brussels, 2002), pp. 3–37, p. 30.

6 Mary Kaldor, 'The Idea of Global Civil Society', *International Affairs*, Vol. 79, pp. 583–93, p. 588.

7 Extract from speech by Prime Minister Thatcher to the Aspen Institute, Colorado, on 5 August 1990, quoted in *Arms Control and Disarmament Quarterly Review* (Foreign and Commonwealth Office, London, 1990), Vol. 19.

8 United Nations Security Council Resolution 660 (1990).

9 United Nations Security Council Resolution 665 (1990).

10 Lawrence Freedman and Efraim Karsh (eds.), *The Gulf Conflict 1990–1991: Diplomacy and War in the New World Order* (Faber and Faber, London), pp. 85–90.

11 *The Economist*, 22 December 1990, p. 80.

12 *Independent*, 6 August 1990, p. 3.

13 Statement by Douglas Hurd, as quoted by Freedman and Karsh (eds.), *The Gulf Conflict 1990–1991*, p. 112.

14 Press Release, British Council of Churches, 16 August 1990; Press Release, Quaker Peace and Service, 16 August 1990; Press Release, Lambeth Palace, 22 August 1990.

15 *House of Lords, Official Report*, 6 September 1990, col. 1809.

16 *The Times*, 7 September 1990, p. 1.

17 Statement by General Schwarzkopf, as quoted by Freedman and Karsh (eds.), *The Gulf Conflict 1990–1991*, p. 204.

18 Statement by President Bush on 9 October 1990, as quoted by Freedman and Karsh (eds.), *The Gulf Conflict 1990–1991*, p. 204.

19 See Dick Cheney's testimony in US Congress, Senate Committee on Armed Services, *Crisis in the Persian Gulf Region: US Policy Options*

and Implications, 3 December 1991, 101 Cong., 2 Session, 1990, p. 649. This position was also shared by the Bishop of Oxford who believed that churches must be 'absolutely adamant that Saddam Hussein must withdraw from Kuwait, and be rendered harmless for future aggression': the Bishop of Oxford as quoted in the *Independent*, 30 October 1990, p. 3.

20 Freedman and Karsh (eds.), *The Gulf Conflict 1990–1991*, p. 219. Freedman shows that there was growing concern within the US Administration even as early as the mid-1980s that Iraq's WMD programme had accelerated to such an extent that the Administration anticipated Iraq would have a nuclear capability within ten years. Freedman indicates that preventing this from occurring had always been a long-term US objective and Iraq's invasion of Kuwait provided the USA with an opportunity to secure it.

21 Powell, *Crisis in the Persian Gulf Region*, p. 672. For figures concerning the financial commitments made by the Gulf States, Japan, Germany and Korea during the early phase of the crisis, see Dick Cheney in *Crisis in the Persian Gulf Region*, p. 426.

22 See the testimony of former Deputy Secretary of State, James Placke, in US Congress, House Committee on Foreign Affairs, *Hearings before the Subcommittee on Europe and the Middle East, Persian Gulf Crisis*, 17 October 1990 (US Government Printing Office, 1991), pp. 269–317.

23 *New York Times*, 9 October 1990, p. 1.

24 Saddam Hussein, 'Address on the Al-Aqsa Incident', *Baghdad Domestic News Service*, 9 October 1990, in FBIS-NES-90-196, pp. 22–3.

25 *New York Times*, 10 October 1990, p. 2; Bob Woodward, *The Commanders* (Simon and Schuster, New York, 1991), p. 298.

26 *House of Commons, Official Report*, 15 January 1991, col. 742.

27 *House of Commons, Official Report*, 15 January 1991, col. 742.

28 United Nations Security Council Resolution 678 (1990).

29 *International Herald Tribune*, 9 November 1990, p. 1.

30 Press Release, Council of Churches for Britain and Ireland, 9 January 1991, p. 3.

31 Press Release, Council of Churches for Britain and Ireland, 9 January 1991, p. 4.

32 Press Release, Council of Churches for Britain and Ireland, 9 January 1991, p. 4.

33 *Sunday Correspondent*, 11 November 1990, p. 3.

34 Press Release, Scottish Episcopal Church, 3 January 1991, p. 2.
35 Press Release, Scottish Episcopal Church, 3 January 1991, p. 2.
36 *The Scotsman*, 4 January 1991, p. 1.
37 Pax Christi, *Just Peace*, No. 150, September 1990, p. 1.
38 Press Release, Irish Council of Churches, 5 January 1991, p. 1.
39 *Guardian*, 5 December 1990, p. 8.
40 General Synod, *Report of Proceedings*, Vol. 21, No. 3, 1990, pp. 926–9, p. 927.
41 General Synod, *Report of Proceedings*, Vol. 21, No. 3, 1990, p. 928.
42 General Synod, *Report of Proceedings*, Vol. 21, No. 3, 1990, p. 927.
43 General Synod, *Report of Proceedings*, Vol. 21, No. 3, 1990, p. 929.
44 *Independent*, 30 October 1990, p. 8.
45 The House of Bishops' statement of 15 January 1991 followed this approach by urging the Government to make sure the issues of proportionality and non-discrimination were central to all political and military thinking, both in the planning and the execution of any military action. *The Gulf Crisis*, Statement by the House of Bishops of the Church of England, 15 January 1991.
46 *The Times*, 8 November 1990, p. 12.
47 'A Message from the Bishops of England and Wales to be read in all Churches on the First Sunday of Advent', 2 December 1990, Catholic Bishops' Conference of England and Wales, 18 November 1990.
48 John Courtney Murray, *We Hold These Truths* (Sheed and Ward, London, 1960), p. 261.
49 Interview with Keith Clements, Secretary General of the Conference of European Churches, June 2003.
50 *Guardian*, 1 November 1990, p. 6; *Church Times*, 11 November 1990, p. 8.
51 As quoted in the *Guardian*, 7 January 1991, p. 7.
52 Philip Crowe and Rowan Williams, 'An Open Letter to the House of Bishops of the Church of England Concerning the Gulf Crisis', 24 March 1991, p. 3; reprinted in the *Church Times*, 28 October, 1991, pp. 3–5. Both Rowan Williams and Philip Crowe wrote subsequent articles on the back of the initiative. *Guardian*, 1 November 1990, p. 12.
53 Crowe and Williams, 'An Open Letter', p. 2.
54 Stephen R. Graubard, *Mr Bush's War: Adventures in the Politics of Illusion* (Hill and Wang, New York, 1992); Jean Edward Smith, *George Bush's War* (Henry Holt, New York, 1992).

55 Douglas Hurd, as quoted by Freedman and Karsh, *The Gulf Conflict 1990–1991*, p. 411.

56 United Nations Security Council Resolution 678 (1990), para, 2.

57 United Nations Security Council Resolution 82 (1950).

58 US Congress, Senate Committee on Armed Services, *Crisis in the Persian Gulf Region*; *Washington Post*, 13 January 1991, p. 1.

59 *Independent*, 24 November 1990, p. 1.

60 *Daily Telegraph*, 11 January 1991, p. 2.

61 *Sunday Times*, 20 January 1991, p. 2.

62 *Church Times*, 11 November 1990, p. 6.

63 *The Times*, 8 November 1990, p. 8.

64 George Bush, 'Remarks by the President in Address to the National Religious Broadcasters Convention', The Sheraton Washington Hotel, Washington DC, 28 January 1991.

65 General H. Norman Schwarzkopf, *It Doesn't Take a Hero* (Bantam Press, London, 1992), p. 421; Air Vice-Marshal R. A. Mason, 'The Air War in the Gulf', *Survival*, Vol. 33, 1991, p. 214.

66 Paul Virilio, *Desert Screen: War at the Speed of Light* (The Athlone Press, New York, 1992), p. viii.

67 *Observer*, 20 January 1991, p. 9.

68 This data is drawn from the USAF White Paper, *Air Force Performance in Desert Storm*, April 1991, as quoted by Edward Luttwark, 'The Air War' in Alex Danchev (ed.), *International Perspectives on the Gulf Crisis, 1990–91* (St Martin's Press, Oxford, 1993), pp. 224–58, p. 229.

69 Luttwark, 'The Air War', pp. 228–9.

70 Schwarzkopf, *It Doesn't Take a Hero*, pp. 468–9; General Sir Peter de la Billiere, *Storm Command: A Personal Account of the Gulf War* (HarperCollins, London, 1992), p. 261.

71 US Department of Defence, *Conduct of the Persian Gulf Conflict: An Interim Report to Congress*, Washington DC, July 1991, pp.12–13.

72 *CENTCOM Briefing*, General Norman Schwarzkopf, Brigadier General Buster Glosson, Riyadh, Saudi Arabia, 30 January 1991.

73 United Nations Security Council, *Report to the Secretary-General on Humanitarian Needs in Kuwait and Iraq in the Immediate Post-Crisis Environment by a Mission to the Area led by Mr Martti Ahtisaari, Under-Secretary-General for Administration and Management*, 10–17 March 1991, S/22366, 29 March 1991, para. 8.

74 *Needless Deaths in the Gulf War: Civilian Casualties during the Air Campaign and Violations of the Laws of War* (Middle East

Watch/Human Rights Watch, New York, 1991); Oscar Schacher, 'United Nations Law in the Gulf Conflict', *American Journal of International Law*, Vol. 85, 1991, p. 466.

75 British officials estimated Iraqi military casualties at 30,000 dead and 100,000 wounded: *Time*, 17 June 1991. This contrasts with figures released by the US Defence Intelligence Agency, which estimated fatalities of 100,000 and 300,000 wounded. William J. Taylor and James Blackwell, 'The Ground War in the Gulf, *Survival*, Vol. 33, 1991, p. 239.

76 In a testimony to the Senate Armed Services Committee on 12 June 1991, General Schwarzkopf gave a total figure of 466 allied fatalities: *The Times*, 13 June 1991, p. 2. This figure includes deaths in all types of circumstances including both those fatalities caused by friendly fire and those fatalities incurred in combat. Other reports place the number of allied fatalities experienced as a result of combat at 138. Taylor and Blackwell, 'The Ground War in the Gulf', p. 239.

77 Adam Roberts, 'The Laws of War' in Danchev (ed.), *International Perspectives*, p. 284.

78 Alexander Haig, *Caveat* (Weidenfeld and Nicolson, London, 1984), p. 125.

79 Text of George Bush's statement as quoted by the *International Herald Tribune*, 1–2 December 1990, p. 2.

80 Press Release, Council of Churches for Britain and Ireland, 17 January 1991.

81 Press Release, Council of Churches for Britain and Ireland, 1 March 1991. Amnesty International issued a similar press release criticizing the Government for allowing the war to lead to an erosion of human rights. AI argued that detention and deportation without a fair judicial hearing and no legal representation was contrary to international law: Press Release, Amnesty International, 8 February 1991, p. 2.

82 Press Release, Lambeth Palace, 17 January 1991.

83 Press Release, Catholic Bishops' Conference of England and Wales, 17 January 1991.

84 Press Release, Quaker Peace and Service, 17 January 1991.

85 CANA Mailing, 23 January 1991.

86 *Independent*, 20 February 1991, p. 7.

87 Pax Christi and Christian CND, *Just Conduct of the War in the Gulf?* (London, February 1991), p. 1.

88 *Independent*, 20 February 1991, p. 7.

89 Roger Williamson, *Engulfed in War: On the Ambivalence of the Just War Tradition and the Political Ineffectiveness of the Churches Peace Wing During the Gulf Crisis.* A study for the Sark M. Matsunga Institute for Peace, University of Hawai'i, April 1991, p. 40.

90 World Council of Churches, Press Release on the Outbreak of Hostilities Against Iraq, Geneva, 17 January 1991.

91 James Turner Johnston and George Weigel (eds.), *Just War and the Gulf War* (The Ethics and Public Policy Centre, Washington DC, 1991), p. 53.

92 'WCC Assembly Calls for Immediate Cease-Fire in Gulf War', Ecumenical Press Service, WCC Seventh Assembly, Canberra, 20 February 1991, p. 2.

93 'WCC Assembly Calls for Immediate Cease-Fire in Gulf War', p. 1.

94 As quoted in the World Council of Churches, *Statement on the Gulf War, the Middle East and the Threat of World Peace*, (WCC, Geneva, 1991), p. 1.

95 'England Clarifies Its Stance', *Assembly Line*, 12 February 1991, p. 1.

96 Statement by the Rt Revd Barry Rogerson, Bishop of Bristol, at a press conference of the World Conference of Churches, Canberra, 11 February 1991.

97 Williamson, *Engulfed in War*, p. 52.

98 United Nations Security Council Resolution 687 (1991).

99 BBC Radio 4, *The Desert War – A Kind of Victory*, 16 February 1992.

100 United Nations Security Council Resolution 688 (1991). In 1993 the remit was widened to set up a southern no-fly zone to protect the Shi'ites in the south of Iraq.

101 Christine Gray, *International Law and the Use of Force* (Oxford University Press, Oxford, 2000), pp. 28–9.

102 'UK Materials on International Law', *British Yearbook of International Law*, Vol. 63, 1992, p. 824.

103 Gray, *International Law and the Use of Force*, p. 30.

104 Press Release, Catholic Bishops' Conference of England and Wales, 12 April 1991.

105 *Guardian*, 2 March 1991, p. 1.

106 As quoted in Freedman and Karsh, *The Gulf Conflict 1990–1991*, p. 426.

107 *Guardian*, 2 March 1991, p. 1.

Chapter 5: Victory without Triumph:
The Second Gulf War, 2001–2003

1 G. John Ikenberry, 'America's Imperial Authority', *Foreign Affairs*, September/October 2002, pp. 44–60, p. 44.

2 *The National Security Strategy of the United States of America*, September 2002, p. 29.

3 *National Security Strategy*, September 2002, p. 2.

4 *National Security Strategy*, September 2002, p. 6.

5 *National Security Strategy*, September 2002, pp. 15–16.

6 *National Security Strategy*, September 2002, pp. 1–2.

7 President George Bush, Address to the United Nations General Assembly, 12 September 2002.

8 President Bush, Cincinnati Speech, 7 October 2002.

9 Bush, Cincinnati Speech.

10 Bush, Cincinnati Speech.

11 Transcript of President Bush and Prime Minister Blair's Press Conference, Washington, 31 January 2003.

12 President George Bush, Address to the Nation, 18 March 2003.

13 United Nations Security Council Resolution 1441, 8 November 2002, paras 1 and 3.

14 United Nations Security Council Resolution 1441, 8 November 2002, para. 2.

15 United Nations Security Council Resolution 1441, 8 November 2002, para. 13

16 Dr Hans Blix, Chairman of UNMOVIC, *An Update on Inspection to the United Nations Security Council*, 27 January 2003, as reproduced in *Iraq: A Report by the Secretary of State for Foreign and Commonwealth Affairs*, February 2003, Cm5769, pp. 67–74, p. 67.

17 Blix, *An Update*, Cm5769, pp. 69–74, p. 69.

18 Blix, *An Update*, Cm5769, pp.79–83, p. 80.

19 Blix, *An Update*, Cm5769, pp. 67–74, p. 69.

20 Blix, *An Update*, Cm5769, pp. 67–74, p. 70.

21 Presentation by Secretary of State Colin Powell to the United Nations Security Council, 6 February 2003.

22 Powell, Presentation, 6 February 2003.

23 Bush, Address to the Nation, 18 March 2003.

24 *National Security Strategy*, September 2002, p. 6.

25 President George Bush, *State of the Union Address*, 28 January 2003.

26 Bush, Address to the UN General Assembly, 12 September 2002.

27 Bush, Address to the Nation, 18 March 2003.

28 Bush, Address to the Nation, 18 March 2003.

29 Statement issued by US President George Bush, UK Prime Minister Tony Blair and Spanish Prime Minister Jose Maria Aznar at their Summit in the Azores, 16 March 2003.

30 United States Conference of Catholic Bishops, Statement on Iraq, 13 November 2003.

31 United States Conference of Catholic Bishops, Statement on Iraq, 13 November 2003.

32 Jack Straw, as quoted in the *Daily Telegraph*, 15 May 2003, p. 12.

33 Prime Minister, Speech at the Foreign Office Conference, 7 January 2003.

34 Prime Minister, Speech at the Foreign Office Conference, 7 January 2003.

35 Prime Minister, Speech at the Foreign Office Conference, 7 January 2003.

36 As quoted in Michael Glennon, 'Why the Security Council Failed', *Foreign Affairs*, Vol. 82, June 2003, pp. 16–35, p. 19.

37 As quoted in Glennon, 'Why the Security Council Failed', p. 20.

38 Conclusions of the European Council, 17 February, 2003, as reproduced in *Iraq: A Report by the Secretary of State for Foreign and Commonwealth Affairs*, February 2003, Cm5769, p. 91.

39 Foreign Secretary's Statement at the UN Security Council, 5, February 2003, as reproduced in *Iraq: A Report*, Cm5769, p. 95.

40 Dominique de Villepin, 'Law, Force and Justice', *International Institute of Strategic Studies*, London, 27 March 2003.

41 CBS interview with President Chirac, 16 March 2003.

42 Memorandum on Iraq by France, Germany and Russia, 24 February 2003.

43 Blix, *An Update*, 22 April 2003.

44 Press Release, Catholic Bishops' Conference of England and Wales, 15 November 2003.

45 Statement by the United Reformed Church, 18 March 2003. Letter from David Coffey, General Secretary of the Baptist Union of Great Britain, to the Prime Minister, 20 September 2002.

46 Statement on Iraq by the United Reformed Church, 10 September 2002.

47 Letter to MPs from the Church of Scotland, 25 September 2003.

48 *Guardian*, 22 February 2003, p. 1.

49 As quoted in the *Guardian*, 22 February 2003, p. 1.

50 'Thought for the Day', BBC Radio 4, 25 March 2003.

51 *Daily Telegraph*, 26 March 2003, p. 6.

52 *A Submission by the House of Bishops to the House of Commons Foreign Affairs Select Committee's Ongoing Inquiry into the War on Terrorism*, October 2002, p. 1.

53 Press Release, Catholic Bishops' Conference of Scotland, 12 February 2003.

54 *House of Lords, Official Report*, 24 September 2002, col. 997.

55 *Submission by the House of Bishops*, p. 19.

56 Press Release, Catholic Bishops' Conference of England and Wales, 15 November 2002.

57 Press Release, Lambeth Palace, February 2003.

58 Press Release, Catholic Theological Association of Great Britain, November 2002.

59 Press Release, Religious Society of Friends, September 2002.

60 Press Release, World Alliance of Reformed Churches, 21 February 2003.

61 *Methodist Church Statement on Iraq*, 21 March 2003.

62 Press Release, Lambeth Palace, February 2003.

63 *House of Lords, Official Report*, 24 September 2002, col. 911.

64 *House of Lords, Official Report*, 24 September 2002, col. 897.

65 Letter from Minister of State Peter Hain to the Rt Revd David Konstant, 16 November 2000.

66 Press Release, Yearly Meeting of the Religious Society of Friends, 3 March 2003.

67 Letter from the Rt Revd Dr Finlay Macdonald to Members of Parliament, 31 August 2002.

68 *General Synod, Report of Proceedings*, Vol. 31, 2000, p. 270.

69 *Methodist Church Statement on Iraq*, 21 March 2003.

70 *House of Lords, Official Report*, 24 September 2002, col. 886.

71 *Iraq Statement, The General Assembly of the Church of Scotland Committee on Church and Nation*, 19 March 2003.

72 *Church of England Newspaper*, 13 February 2003, p. 9.

73 Press Release, United Reformed Church, 18 March 2003; The Bishop of Hereford as quoted in the *Daily Telegraph*, 26 March 2003, p. 6.

74 *House of Lords, Official Report*, 17 March 2003, cols 79–80.

75 Press Release, House of Bishops, 12 January 2003.

76 Archbishop Rowan Williams, 'The End of War? Further Reflections after 9/11', Sarum College, 3 October 2002, p. 8.

77 *Observer*, 2 August 2002, p. 6.

78 Interview, 5 June 2003.

79 Interview, 22 June 2003.

80 Interview, 5 June 2003.

81 Harlan Ullman, 'Shock and Awe Revisited', *RUSI Journal*, June 2003, Vol. 148, pp. 10–14, p. 10.

82 Michael Codner, 'An Initial Assessment of the Combat Phase' in Jonathan Eyal (ed.), *War in Iraq: Combat and Consequences*, RUSI Whitehall Paper 59, pp. 7–26, p. 13.

83 Codner, 'Initial Assessment', p. 14.

84 Ullman, 'Shock and Awe Revisited', p. 11.

85 US Department of Defence Press Briefing, 20 March 2003.

86 Air Vice-Marshal Ian McNicoll, 'Effects Based Operations: Air Command and Control and the Nature of the Emerging Battle-space', *RUSI Journal*, Vol. 148, June 2003, pp. 38–43, p. 39.

87 Presentation by Paul Hirs, 'Twenty First Century Warfare', at the RUSI/*Guardian* Whitehall Security Seminar, 'Future Weaponry', 19 May 2003.

88 Lietenant General Michael Mosely, *Operation Iraqi Freedom – By the Numbers*, USCENTAF, May 2003, pp. 6–8.

89 *Financial Times*, 30 May 2003, p. 2.

90 Codner, 'Initial Assessment', p. 18.

91 Christopher Coker, *Empires in Conflict: The Growing Rift Between Europe and the United States*, RUSI Whitehall Paper 58, 2003, p. 32.

92 *Church Times*, 28 March 2003, p. 2.

93 Major Charles Heyman, 'The Intelligent Battlefield' at the RUSI/*Guardian* Whitehall Security Seminar, 'Future Weaponry', 19 May 2003.

94 *Church Times*, 21 March 2003, p. 9.

95 *Church Times*, 28 March 2003, p. 3.

96 *The Tablet*, 29 March 2003, pp. 29–30, p. 29.

97 *Daily Telegraph*, 21 March 2003, p. 3.

98 BBC Radio 4 *Sunday* programme, 23 March 2003; *Guardian* 24 March 2003, p. 13; *Observer*, 23 March 2003 p. 5; *Independent* 24 March 2003, p. 4.

99 *Church Times*, 21 March 2003, p. 9.

100 *The Times*, 19 April 2003, p. 10.

101 *Church Times*, 11 April 2003, p. 1.

102 *Guardian*, 5 April 2003, p. 12.

103 *The Times*, 3 April 2003, p. 16.

104 *The Times*, 24 March 2003, p. 6.

105 *The Times*, 21 March 2003, p. 9.

106 *The Times*, 21 March 2003, p. 23.

107 *Independent*, 22 March 2003, p. 24.

108 *Church Times*, 28 March 2003, p. 3.

109 *The Times*, 3 March 2003, p. 1.

110 Press Statement, Lambeth Palace, 21 March 2003.

111 *Guardian*, 26 March 2003, p. 24.

112 *Guardian*, 26 March 2003, p. 24.

113 *Church Times*, 4 April 2003, p. 9.

114 *Church Times*, 18 April 2003, p. 8.

115 *The Times*, 22 April 2003, p. 6.

116 *Financial Times*, 19 April 2003, p. 2.

117 Minxin Pei, 'Lessons of the Past' in *From Victory to Success: Afterwar Policy in Iraq*, Foreign Policy and Carnegie Endowment Special Report, Washington, July 2002, pp. 52–5. See also Minxin Pei and Sarah Kasper's policy brief, *Lessons from the Past: The American Record of Nation Building* (Carnegie Endowment, Washington, 2003).

118 Minxin Pei, 'Lessons of the Past', p. 55.

119 These assurances were given following a summit between Blair and Bush at Hillsborough Castle in Northern Ireland on 8 April 2003.

120 United Nations Security Council Resolution 1483, 22 May 2003.

121 Gareth Stansfield, 'Politics and Governance in the New Iraq: Reconstruction of the New Versus Resurrection of the Old' in Eyal (ed.), *War in Iraq*, p. 72.

122 General Dan Christman, former Pentagon planner, as quoted in *The Times*, 12 July, 2003, p. 6.

123 *IRIN News*, 12 May 2003.

124 Rather than increasing its military presence in Iraq the Bush Administration, as early as May 2003, expressed hopes that its military presence would be cut from 146,000 troops to between 30,000 and 40,000.

125 *The Times*, 16 July 2003, p. 13.

126 Marina Ottaway, 'One Country, Two Plans' in *From Victory to Success*, p. 59.

127 Interview by the Archbishop of Westminster, Cardinal Cormac Murphy-O'Connor, speaking on ITV's *The Sunday Programme*, 1 July 2003.

128 House of Commons Foreign Affairs Committee, *The Decision to Go*

to War in Iraq, Ninth Report of session 2002–03, Vols I–II, HC 813–1.

129 Speech by Donald Rumsfeld in New York to the Council on Foreign Relations, 29 May 2003, as quoted by the *Independent*, 29 May 2003, p. 6.

130 Statement by Jack Straw on the BBC's Today programme on 14 May 2003, as quoted in the *Independent*, 29 May, 2003, p. 6.

131 As quoted in the *Sunday Telegraph*, 1 June 2003, p. 1.

132 As quoted in the *Independent*, 29 May 2003, p. 6.

133 *Independent*, 2 June 2003, p. 13.

134 House of Commons Foreign Affairs Committee, *The Decision to Go to War in Iraq*, p. 6.

135 House of Commons Foreign Affairs Committee, *The Decision to Go to War in Iraq*, p. 4.

136 House of Commons Foreign Affairs Committee, *The Decision to Go to War in Iraq*, p. 3.

137 Robin Cook raised this question in his evidence to the House of Commons Foreign Affairs Committee. House of Commons Foreign Affairs Committee, *The Decision to Go to War in Iraq*, HC 813.

138 Church of England Submission to the House of Commons Foreign Affairs Committee, *The Decision to Go to War in Iraq*, HC 813–1, Ev. 22, p. 10.

139 House of Commons Foreign Affairs Committee, *The Decision to Go to War in Iraq*, HC 813-1, Ev. 22.

140 House of Commons Foreign Affairs Committee, *The Decision to Go to War in Iraq*, HC 813–1, Ev. 22. A poll by the *Daily Telegraph* on 2 June 2003 showed that 44 per cent of those polled believed that Prime Minister Blair and President Bush had misled them regarding the threat from Iraq's weapons of mass destruction. Whereas before the war 71 per cent of the public were prepared to believe that Iraq possessed chemical and biological weapons, that proportion dropped to 51 per cent.

141 *The National Security Strategy of the United States of America*, September 2002, p. 2.

142 Alex Danchev, 'Greeks and Romans: Anglo-American Relations after 9/11', *RUSI Journal*, April 2003, Vol. 148, pp. 16–19, p. 19.

143 Glennon, 'Why the Security Council Failed', p. 28.

144 *Financial Times*, 9 July 2003, p. 19.

Chapter 6: Postscript

1   Francis Fukuyama, *The End of History and the Last Man* (Hamish Hamilton, London, 1992).

2   Douglas Klusmeyer and Astri Suhrke, 'Comprehending "Evil": Challenges for Law and Policy', *Ethics and International Affairs*, Vol. 16, 2002, pp. 22–45, p. 27; Roland Bieber, 'A Rogue is a Rogue is a Rogue: US Foreign Policy and the Korean Nuclear Crisis', *International Affairs*, Vol. 79, 2003, pp. 719–38.

3   Bieber; 'A Rogue', pp. 719–38.

4   CNN, 6 November 2001.

5   Max Boot, 'The New American Way of War', *Foreign Affairs*, Vol. 82, July 2003, pp. 41–59, p. 44.

6   Major Charles Heyman, 'The Intelligent Battlefield' at the RUSI/*Guardian* Whitehall Security Seminar, 'Future Weaponry', 19 May 2003, p. 2.

7   Michael Codner, 'Hanging Together: Military Interoperability in an Era of Technological Innovation', *The Royal United Services Institute for Defence Studies*, Whitehall Paper 56, 2003, p. 27.

8   Charles Krauthammer, 'The Unipolar Moment', *Foreign Affairs*, October 1990, pp. 22–33; Christopher Lane, 'The Unipolar Illusion: Why New Great Powers Will Arise', *International Security*, Spring 1993, 5–51; Charles Kupchan, 'After Pax Americana: Benign Power, Regional Integration and the Sources of Stable Multipolarity', *International Security*, Fall 1998.

9   Joseph Nye, *The Paradox of American Power: Why the World's Only Superpower Can't Go It Alone* (Oxford University Press, Oxford, 2002).

10 Robert Kagan, *Paradise and Power: America and Europe in the New World Order* (Atlantic Books, London, 2003).

11 Kagan, *Paradise and Power*, pp. 3–4.

12 Kagan, *Paradise and Power*, p. 61.

13 Press Release, United Reformed Church, 10 September 2002.

14 As quoted in Kagan, *Paradise and Power*, p. 61.

Index